# ABCs of an Author/Illustrator Visit

## 2nd Edition

## Sharron L. McElmeel

A Publication of THE BOOK REPORT & LIBRARY TALK
Professional Growth Series

Linworth Publishing, Inc.
Worthington, Ohio

*For Jack, whose partnership makes all things happen, and for all of the authors and illustrators who have made things happen for children.*

All photographs by Sharron L. McElmeel, reprinted with the permission of the author.

McElmeel, Sharron L.
    ABCs of an author/illustrator visit / by Sharron L. McElmeel.—2nd ed.
      p. cm.
    Includes bibliographical references and index.
    ISBN 1-58683-034-1
     1. Children's libraries—Activity programs—United States. 2. School libraries—Activity programs—United States. 3. Children—Books and reading—United States. 4. Authors, American. I. Title.

Z718.1 .M367 2001
027.8'222'0973—dc21

2001029295

Published by Linworth Publishing, Inc.
480 East Wilson Bridge Road, Suite L
Worthington, Ohio 43085

Copyright © 2001 by Linworth Publishing, Inc.

Series Information:
    From The Professional Growth Series

All rights reserved. Reproduction of this book in whole or in part is prohibited without written permission of the publisher. Permission is granted to the purchaser of this book to duplicate applicable forms on pages 90-106 for use within a single building or institution (library, museum, and so forth ) in conjunction with a planned author focus.

ISBN 1-58683-034-1

5 4 3 2 1

# Table of Contents

INTRODUCTION .................................................................................................. iii

**SECTION 1:**     **BENEFITS OF AN AUTHOR/ILLUSTRATOR VISIT** ............................................. 1
- Is This a Great Idea or What? ........................................................... 1
- Discussing the Benefits .................................................................... 3
- Gathering Support .......................................................................... 5
  - A Multitude of Benefits ............................................................... 5

**SECTION 2:**     **GETTING ORGANIZED** ................................................................................ 7
- Establishing the Committee ............................................................. 7
- Funding the Event .......................................................................... 8
- How Much Money Will It Take ......................................................... 9
- Where Will the Money Come From? ............................................... 11
- A Blueprint for a Community-Wide Reading Initiative ..................... 12
- Identifying Possible Cosponsors .................................................... 14
- Involving Cosponsors ................................................................... 16

**SECTION 3:**     **MAKING DECISIONS** ............................................................................... 19
- What Type of Visit Should You Plan? ............................................. 19
  - The One-Day, One-Host Event .................................................. 19
  - Young Author's Day ................................................................. 19
  - Children's Literature Festivals and Conferences ........................ 20
  - Multi-Day, Multi-Host Visit ....................................................... 21
- When Will the Event Take Place .................................................... 22
  - Choosing a Date ...................................................................... 23
- Choosing an Author/Illustrator ...................................................... 24
  - Creating an Environment for Participation ................................ 27
  - Making a List of Possibilities .................................................... 30
  - Extending the Invitation ........................................................... 32
  - Getting It in Writing ................................................................. 38
- Where Should You Hold the Event? ............................................... 40
  - Function of the Facility ............................................................. 42
  - Microphones and Sound Systems ............................................. 43
  - Technology .............................................................................. 43
  - Lunch and Amenities ............................................................... 44

**SECTION 4:**     **THE AUTHOR/ILLUSTRATOR FOCUS** ........................................................ 47
- Importance of Preparing the Audience ........................................... 47
- Planning the Focus ....................................................................... 48
- Collaborating to Make Connections ............................................... 49
- Preparing a Resource Booklet ....................................................... 50
  - Building on the Ideas of Others ................................................ 50
  - Using Book Webs .................................................................... 52
- Bring on the Books ....................................................................... 53
- Introducing the Focus ................................................................... 54
- Getting Ready in Other Settings .................................................... 55
- Using Videos and Books About Authors/Illustrators ....................... 56
  - Authors on Video ..................................................................... 57
- Books About Authors and Illustrators ............................................ 59
- Author and Illustrator Web Sites as a Resource ............................. 61
  - Authors and Illustrators on the Web ......................................... 62
  - One Connection for 25 or More Students .................................. 63
  - Researching and Sharing the Information ................................. 63
- Reading Motivation ...................................................................... 64

**SECTION 5:**     **MAKING THE DAY SHINE** ....................................................................... 65
- Scheduling the Day ...................................................................... 65
  - Sample Schedule ..................................................................... 66
  - Avoiding the Pitfalls ................................................................ 66
- Obtaining Books for Autographing Sessions .................................. 66
  - Do It Yourself, Or "Contracting" the Book Sales ........................ 67
- Making the Guest of Honor Welcome ............................................ 68
- What Questions Will You Ask? ...................................................... 70

# Table of Contents continued

        Finding Out the Obvious Before the Visit .......................... 70
        A Few Guidelines .......................................... 70
    Opportunities to Promote Reading and Your School or Organization ........... 71
    Photographing the Day's Activities .................................. 71
        Keeping an Eye on the Objective ............................... 71
        Digital or Prints? .......................................... 72
        Video — Is It Worth It? ..................................... 72
        Sharing the Photos ........................................ 73
    Providing a Personal Host ....................................... 73
    Restroom Facilities and Related Considerations ......................... 74
    Book Sales .................................................. 74
    Autographing Sessions ......................................... 75
    Providing a Keepsake for All Children ............................... 78
    Emergency Box ............................................... 78
    The Big Day ................................................. 78

**SECTION 6:**   **AFTER THE VISIT** ............................................ 79
    Things to Do ................................................. 79
    Evaluation — How Did the Visit Go? ................................ 80
    A Final Word ................................................ 80
        To the Visiting Artist ...................................... 80
        To The Sponsors ......................................... 81
        To Others Who Contributed Time, Ideas, and Support ............... 81

**SECTION 7:**   **NO EXCUSES** ............................................... 83
    Visits Using Communications Networks .............................. 84
    Online Visits ................................................. 84
    U.S. Mail or E-mail ............................................ 85
    Bookstore Visits .............................................. 86
    Museums and Art Centers ....................................... 87

**SECTION 8:**   **FORMS** .................................................... 89
    Form 1: Benefits of an Author/Illustrator Focus ......................... 90
    Form 2: Author/Illustrator Visit: Checklist and Time Line .................. 91
    Form 3: Budget Worksheet ...................................... 93
    Form 4: Accounting Log ........................................ 94
    Form 5: Statement: Expenses and Honoraria ......................... 95
    Form 6: Worksheet: Search for Possible Grants or Cosponsors ............. 96
    Form 7: Worksheet: Tentative Dates for the Author/Illustrator Visit .......... 97
    Form 8: Worksheet: Author/Illustrator Appearance ...................... 98
    Form 9: Phone Log ............................................ 99
    Form 10: Directory Information Inquiry Log .......................... 100
    Form 11: Making the Most of an Author/Illustrator Visit (A Newsletter) ....... 101
    Form 12: Sample Floor Plan for Book Sales .......................... 103
    Form 13: Sample Book Order for an Author/Illustrator Visit ............... 104
    Form 14: Autograph Forms for School Visits .......................... 105
    Form 15: Autograph Forms for Non-school Visits ....................... 106

**SECTION 9:**   **RESOURCES** .............................................. 107
    Videos About Authors and Illustrators ............................... 108
        Retrospective List ........................................ 108
        Current List of Author/Illustrator Videos ........................ 109
    Books About Authors and Illustrators ............................... 113
    Selected Sources of Author Videos ................................ 115
    Selected Sources of Children's and Young Adult Literature and Resources
        About Authors and Illustrators ............................... 115
    World Wide Web Author/Illustrator Resources ........................ 118
        Gateways to Information about Authors and Illustrators on the Web ...... 118
        Author/Illustrator Web Sites ................................. 118

**AUTHOR/ILLUSTRATOR INDEX** ........................................... 120

**ABOUT THE AUTHOR** .................................................. 122

# Introduction

When this book was published in 1994, *Booklist* said, "This volume really does take readers through the ins and outs of an author/illustrator visit. Everything is covered. Good idea, good execution."

Needless to say, I was pleased. Seven years later, however, there are aspects of an author/illustrator visit that were not covered in that first edition. The World Wide Web has brought us new options for locating information, sharing ideas, and connecting with authors and illustrators. New artists have arrived on the scene, and we have a new awareness of how they motivate reading. Entire school districts, like the Chicago Public Schools, have embarked on well-thought-out plans to bring authors or illustrators into elementary schools. They have conducted workshops to help library media specialists and classroom teachers develop strategies for working together to focus on an author/illustrator, and then the district has provided a stipend to help fund the artist's visit.

In this revised edition, readers will find new suggestions for coping with the higher cost of bringing an author/illustrator to a community. Every section of the book has updated and additional information. While I have kept most of the section titles and subheadings, readers will find expanded ideas and references in each section. I have added current titles to resource lists. First-edition readers will find new anecdotes, new authors and illustrators to consider, and updated information all around. The basic principles of a well-planned focus event remain the same, however. Those who are reading the book for the first time will, we are confident, find it a valuable resource for connecting authors, illustrators, books, and young readers.

Focusing on an author/illustrator to motivate reading will be only as successful as the effort that goes into preparing for the event. The focus, which is independent of the actual visit, can promote a book creator and can be culminated in a number of ways, but always with a special activity intended to celebrate the joy of reading and sharing the author's or illustrator's books. Making that activity an actual visit by the author/illustrator will produce immeasurable benefits.

One year I organized a multi-day author residency by Craig Brown in several schools. At the time, he was not especially well known. He certainly lacked the stature of a Steven Kellogg, for example. However, as a result of a carefully planned residency, young readers in our school from kindergarten through fifth grade came to love and enjoy Brown's picture books. He became one of their most popular artists.

In fact, after several years we heard younger students refer to Craig Brown as a personal friend—students who hadn't even been in the school when he visited. They were catching the excitement and popularity generated by his visit from older siblings and friends. Several years after his visit, seeing a Brown illustration on the library media center wall, first graders commented, "Remember when *he* visited our school? What's your favorite book?" Eventually, we decided to invite Brown back for a repeat visit so that the younger students could meet their favorite author.

For several years, I had been involved in planning and hosting a district-sponsored children's literature conference for adults. The conference, always exciting, furnished me with information and tidbits to take back to my school. But my enthusiasm for bringing that same experience directly to children began with a school visit from Beatrice Schenk de Regniers, who charmed adults and children alike with her reading of her simple book *Going for a Walk* (HarperCollins, 1982). I saw how such a picture book could appeal to many ages. The students adored her, and she seemed to adore them.

Before her visit, the children sent her materials telling about their city and school, where they lived, and their daily lives. She came prepared to tell them about her city (New York), her favorite places (including Central Park), and what she did on a typical day. She took time to read some of the books the students had written, and she answered questions. She talked about the importance of reading and learning. When she left at the end of the day, the children felt as though they had been involved in a very special activity. For weeks they continued to bask in the sunshine created by her visit.

For several years those who had been fortunate enough to meet de Regniers passed on their joyous response to her books. Teachers continued to feature this author in focus units, and the students introduced her books to their younger brothers and sisters, read them aloud to younger reading-buddies, and told new students about the great author they had met. de Regniers' books were always checked out, but the children's enthusiasm for reading went beyond her books. They continued to look for connections between books and authors. They searched for new versions of stories, created thematic webs, and researched information that would collaborate the facts they were discovering in their reading. The continued benefits of this author's day validated all the work and energy that went into the planning and provided the inspiration for many more author events to come.

A few years later, while another school was preparing for a visit from David Wisniewski, I observed children in the library media center reading his books, looking at the pictures of authors and illustrators who had visited their school in the past, and talking about their likes and dislikes. They spoke of the books they read and of the new books they were becoming acquainted with. They discussed Wisniewski's cut-paper illustrations and marveled at their beauty. They came back several times to finish reading *Sundiata* (Clarion, 1993).

More recently, I have seen young readers seek out the poems from Ashley Bryan's *ABC of African American Poetry* (Jean Karl/Atheneum, 1997) and then observed the delight of their classroom teacher and Ashley Bryan when three third graders asked permission to share a poem with him. They regaled their schoolmates with a perfectly rehearsed choral recitation of one of their favorite poems from his book.

Imagine the pride when our students realized that one of our favorite local authors, Jacqueline Briggs Martin, had actually read us an early version of the book *Snowflake Bentley* (Houghton Mifflin, 1998), which went on to become the 1999 Caldecott Award book for its wonderful illustrations by Mary Azarian. Just listening to their enthusiasm made me aware once more that all the work of planning author/illustrator focus units and visits is worth it.

The goal of this edition is the same as that of the earlier edition: to share some of the excitement of author and illustrator visits, to discuss pitfalls to avoid, and to provide detailed help for planning an author/illustrator day in your community.

*Sharron L. McElmeel*

# SECTION 1

# Benefits of an Author/Illustrator Visit

## ▶ IS THIS A GREAT IDEA OR WHAT?

Three third-grade girls stand in front of 200 of their classmates and share a choral recitation of a poem about Harriet Tubman, then bask in the applause that follows. Their inspiration? A visit in which Ashley Bryan introduced them to his collection of African-American poetry. Hearing one stanza of one of the poems started them on a three-week search for the full poem and led them to books about the poem's subject, Harriet Tubman. They became experts on this heroic person, an interest eventually extending to the whole topic of the Underground Railroad. Their confidence in their ability to gather information about a subject of interest continues to fuel their passion for learning about new topics.

A second-grade class, reading David McPhail's "pig" books, create their own life-sized scene from one of the books. They write and read and draw and sing. They have a focus and make connections. And then there are the conversations—the wonderful conversations.

The scene in the library media center was a familiar one. Three intermediate students (all boys) were sitting around a table browsing through *Sundiata* by David Wisniewski (Clarion, 1993). Their conversation centered on the "awesome" illustrations and the story's setting.

"How do you think he did that?"

"Hey, it says this guy (Sundiata) lived 800 years ago."

"When is the author coming?"

"Do we get to ask him questions?"

### ASHLEY BRYAN
*Ashley Bryan's ABC of African American Poetry*
*Ashley Bryan's African Tales, Uh-Huh*
*Beat the Story-Drum, Pum-Pum*

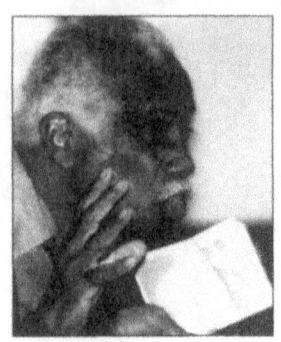

Ashley Bryan lives on a little island off the coast of Maine, an island he discovered years ago while he was a college student. When he visits schools, he recites some of his favorite poems, poems by Langston Hughes, Paul Laurence Dunbar, Eloise Greenfield, and Gwendolyn Brooks. Reciting poems and stories from his own books, Bryan helps young readers find the emotion inherent in the written and spoken word. He holds the book so the listeners connect his words with the printed version.

---

"I really like it when we get to talk to the guys who write these."

Soon the conversation turned to our "authors' gallery," photos of authors and illustrators who had visited our school in past years. It was clear from their animated conversation that these fifth graders enjoyed the visits and had read many different books as a result of past author and illustrator visits. We had just begun the focus for this year's guest, and already these boys were geared up to read and welcome David Wisniewski to our school.

In the past dozen or so years, I have heard similar conversations many times. I have observed children put on their best behavior and their best clothing to meet "the author." They have come to school excited to be part of the activities that surround the visit. It's difficult to know what long-lasting effect such events have on readers, but when I encounter students from past years, one of the first things they mention to me is the book or books they are currently reading and the author and illustrator who created the book. In all probability their interest in reading is due not only to the artists' visits but to the entire program, which depends heavily on author/illustrator focus units to motivate reading and other literacy activities. An author/illustrator visit is a most effective way to culminate a unit.

More than 25 years ago, when I invited some of the first authors and illustrators to our community, it was an innovative, novel idea. Since that time, the idea has flourished. In some years alone, our community (a metropolitan area anchored by a city of 100,000 residents) has held more than 15 author and illustrator events. Some visits were in connection with large conferences. Other visits were associated with schools, college courses, and young writers' conferences.

Enthusiasm has grown because those who work with young readers see benefits. The visits inspire educators and motivate young readers. The benefits are difficult to quantify, but we can see the enthusiasm. We can feel the excitement. And we can observe the renewed interest in learning more about settings, events, and literacy activities.

Our community was involved in a month-long focus on reading and "Building a Community of Readers," an event that involved the cooperation of all the area's school districts, public libraries, art museums, science centers, history centers, and many civic organizations. The cooperative efforts brought to our community a national ALA reading and mathematics exhibit, "Go Figure," and author visits by Loreen Leedy, Jane Kurtz, E. B. Lewis, Herman Parish, and several others, including several storytellers.

Because bringing living, breathing authors and illustrators together with their young readers has been a success in our community and many others, author and illustrator visits have become a growth business in the last 15 years. Adults who work with young readers are convinced that inviting writers and artists to visit is a powerful motivator, that an author/illustrator day in their community is a great idea. Many schools are creating line item budget accounts for such visits; other districts are promoting each school's involvement in the events. In Chicago more than 300 educators, classroom teachers, and library media specialists gathered to learn strategies for collaborating to make an author/illustrator visit successful. Their fledgling efforts were rewarded with district funds to help with the costs involved.

Those who have never experienced an author/illustrator visit will have many questions. What makes it so great? Do we want to try to do this? How do we convince others to join in the planning? How complicated will the planning be? How expensive is getting an author/illustrator to visit? And most important, will the benefits be worth all the effort?

When a school or other organization begins to think about sponsoring an author/illustrator day, the first concern is support for the idea itself. The idea must eventually belong to a substantial portion of the staff of a school or organization. It must become a consensus idea. But a firm commitment or great idea seldom occurs to members of a group simultaneously. It takes a catalyst to turn an idea into a consensus—a person who sells the idea to others, garnering support. That catalyst might be the librarian, a teacher, administrator, or member of a support organization such as the parent-teacher organization or friends of the public library. If you are reading this book, you are likely a prime candidate for becoming a catalyst. Some of the charts and quick lists in this book will help you entice others who are less inclined to read an entire book to join in your enthusiasm and help move the process along.

## ▶ DISCUSSING THE BENEFITS

The benefits of a visit will be your major selling point to persuade colleagues to promote and support an author/illustrator day. Begin by talking about the idea, informally, with your colleagues. Find out if anyone else in your organization is interested. Bring up the idea over lunch or during long-range planning sessions or committee meetings. Make connections with others who may be interested. When you attend a conference, share information about authors and illustrators you have met and how you are using that experience to get your own students involved with books and reading.

The concept of hosting an author/illustrator must have the support of those who will be involved in preparing for the event. The planning and enthusiasm for an author/illustrator day will probably begin with a core group of people eager to provide this type of experience for their own students or to help other educators learn more about the process of writing and illustrating books for young readers. If they are familiar with the

**Nothing creates more enthusiasm than your own enthusiasm.**

benefits of an author/illustrator event, their support, I believe, will be easy to come by. But it will be up to you, as catalyst, to discuss the benefits.

Author/illustrator visits most often come about in one of three ways.

**1** One or two people on the staff have talked with other professionals about an author/illustrator visit and wish to provide a similar experience for their own students.

**2** Several staff members think an author/illustrator visit might be a good idea but need more information before they are willing to commit time and energy.

**3** Most of the staff have seen the benefits of a writer's or artist's visit and want to repeat the experience.

The best of all situations is the third, but most often it is one person or a small group of people who initially are interested in promoting an author/illustrator day. To have ample support for a visit, those interested people must spread the word and kindle enthusiasm.

That is exactly what happened in one elementary school. A couple of staff members talked to colleagues who had been involved in an author/illustrator visit and became convinced that inviting a writer or illustrator to their own school would have benefits for their children. They initiated a proposal to the rest of the staff. After some general discussions concerning benefits for the students, the staff incorporated the idea of a visit into their school improvement plan and in general expressed support. They listed their preferences as to what time of year to hold the event and what type of author/illustrator to invite. As their interest grew, participation in the planning sessions grew as well—enough that the administrator, library media specialist, and three staff members were named to the planning committee.

After conferring with a publishing house publicist, the committee proceeded to schedule

> ★ The author visit was so successful that, in an evaluative report to the board of education, the principal wrote, "In my 25 years as a principal I have never seen more success in getting children to read, and most important, to enjoy reading. The author visit made reading a high priority, and such fun, with both staff and students at our school. In conjunction with the proposed author unit activity, suggestions were developed that included expressive arts, writing motivation, collaborative readings, creative dramatics, bookmaking, and much more—all activities to correlate with the author's books. The actual author visit was a tremendous success. The enthusiasm among the students and staff was beyond all expectations."

Beatrice Schenk de Regniers. A half-year in advance, they set a November date for her visit. During summer curriculum planning sessions, they prepared suggestions for an author focus, created a promotional blitz to acquaint all the teachers with the author's work, and developed promotional and response activities aimed directly at the students.

When school resumed in the fall, the library media specialist, in curriculum planning sessions with teachers, concentrated on identifying ways the author's books could be incorporated into curriculum goals. The planners realized that it was important that the goals of focus activities correspond with goals and objectives already identified by teachers and their students. The planning sessions helped teachers bring information about de Regniers into the classroom and plan activities focusing on the author and her work. The author focus was school-wide and began during the first few weeks of the school year. As classrooms began to exhibit some of their artwork, writings, and other visual displays relating to de Regniers' books, enthusiasm grew. The day de Regniers arrived could not have been more exciting.

The publicist who had helped arrange the visit wrote, "Beatrice de Regniers reported that her visit was the most inspiring of all her school visits. She was so impressed with how much the teachers care about their children and in turn by how responsive the children were. She was equally delighted with the display of children's artwork and the writing relating to her books that lined the classroom walls. Thank you for all your efforts to make it such a successful trip."

The author herself wrote, "I want to thank all of you for the wonderful reception you gave me when I came to your school. I keep thinking about all the people I met, all the beautiful artwork I saw, and all the written work. Every day I remember more interesting things that happened. I have been telling my husband about all of you, and he is interested and impressed. I told him about the big welcome banners all over the school. When I told him about the great giants in the hallways, he said, 'Why didn't you bring one home to show me?' (I'm sorry I didn't.)

"Then I told Francis—that's my husband's name—about the ice cream served for lunch and about all the clocks in the cafeteria set at 3 o'clock. It just happens that of all my books Francis's favorite is *How Joe the Bear and Sam the Mouse Got Together*. So, of course, he thought the idea of the ice cream and the clocks was a neat one."

She continued to mention more of the things she observed during her visit and the student books she had read; throughout her letter, she mentioned names of children and classrooms. Her final words were "I know there will be even more things I will

## BEATRICE SCHENK DE REGNIERS
*How Joe the Bear and Sam the Mouse Got Together*
*What Can You Do With a Shoe?*
*May I Bring a Friend?*

Beatrice Schenk de Regniers's books were the essence of simplicity but had universal appeal. Her own soft, gentle nature endeared her to all she met, children and adults alike. Among favorite stories was her retelling of *Little Sister and the Month Brothers*, in which she included elements from her own childhood—her love of strawberries and the abundance of violets in the grassy fields near her home. Beatrice Schenk de Regniers was born in Lafayette, Indiana, but lived in her adopted city, New York, in an apartment near Central Park, for more than 50 years. She died there on March 1, 2000. In recent years, several of her books have been re-issued with new illustrations.

remember about you as time goes by. I really think I will never forget you."

In following years, planning committees planned and executed additional author events. Some members stayed on the committee while others relinquished their places to new volunteers. Committee members used their experiences to make each author event better than the last. By getting as many of the staff involved as they could, they generated enthusiasm that continued to grow.

The committee invited local authors Jacqueline Briggs Martin and Carol Gorman as well as other writers and illustrators to visit the school to talk about their books. In conjunction with a local reading association's spring award banquet, they invited Robert Burch to spend a day at the school. The next year, funding from the local area education agency helped to sponsor a school visit from Gloria Skurzynski in conjunction with an evening presentation for area educators. Each visit brought a new set of books into the school experience. Each guest author's books were compared and contrasted with other titles with similar themes or plots. Collaborative reading encouraged young readers to make their own connections, to explore their own threads of understanding, and to share those connections with their classmates. Students responded to the literature they read with visual, musical, and dance creations, and each gained the priceless legacy of enthusiasm for reading and writing.

## ▶ GATHERING SUPPORT

The planning committee for the author/illustrator day will need to assess and gain support within its own school, public library, college department, or community. Members undoubtedly will be asked about the benefits of an author/illustrator visit.

A list of the benefits most often mentioned by those who have hosted writers and artists in their community follows. As with many other activities, it is not only the final product that is important but

---

### ROBERT BURCH
*Ida Early Comes Over the Mountain*
*Christmas with Ida Early*
*Queenie Peavy*

"I'm happy that many of you have read *Christmas with Ida Early*. I hope you enjoyed it. Someday I want to write another story about Ida and the Sutton children, and I wish you could help me decide on a title for it. It will be called either *Valentines for Ida Early* or *Ida Early Gives Lessons on Love*. You could also help me decide what should happen in the story. Someone has suggested that Ida might marry the young preacher who is in *Christmas with Ida Early*, but I'm thinking that in the next book I may send the preacher off as a missionary halfway around the world! Someone else suggested that Ida marry Mr. Sutton. I believe they'll always be friends, but I don't really think they should get married, do you? Perhaps I should invent a new character who'll be just right for Ida. How would that be?"

— Robert Burch

---

also the process of getting there. In the case of an author/illustrator day, the day itself is a culminating event in the process of becoming acquainted with a new literary connection. The learning and activity that precede it are an integral part of the day.

This benefits list may be useful when you discuss the pros and cons of an author/illustrator day with administrators or others whose time, energy, cooperation, or financial support may be vital to the event's success. Later in the process, you might use the list in a formal solicitation presentation. Section 8, p.90 (Form 1) includes this chart in a large-print format that you can reproduce as a transparency master or as a handout to stimulate discussions about the benefits.

### *A Multitude of Benefits*

An author/illustrator visit:
- Motivates reading and writing and other responses to literature.
- Gives young readers a positive experience with reading and writing.
- Builds enthusiasm for an in-depth experience with literary selections.
- Puts reading and writing in the spotlight—on an equal basis with sports and music events.
- Provides opportunities for audience responses to reading.

## CYNTHIA RYLANT
*When I Was Young in the Mountains*
*The Relatives Came*
*Henry and Mudge and the Big Sleep Over*
*Tulip Sees America*

"My teacher knows all about Cynthia Rylant. Her books are good. She lived in the mountains with her grandmother and grandfather when she was little. We read *When I Was Young in the Mountains*. She really did put a black snake around her neck. We got to put a pin in the mountains where she lived. She lives in Ohio now. We put a pin there too. Nate lives there, too. He's her son. They don't have Mudge any more but they used to. Now they have little dogs. I really like her books. I want to get [the book] *Henry and Mudge*. Mudge is a dog."

— Ryan (age 7)

In 1993, Rylant and her friend, author and illustrator Dav Pilkey, moved to Oregon. The move resulted in Rylant's *Tulip Sees America*. On his Web site <http://www.pilkey.com>, Dav Pilkey includes limited information about his friend, Cynthia Rylant, and the move to Oregon.

---

- Produces opportunities for developing planning skills and cooperative learning.
- Offers a structure for the sharing of literature—a structure that allows for the organization of activities and a time to read in such a way as to provide for the achievement of curriculum or program goals.
- Develops a respect for the body of work of a writer or illustrator.
- Demonstrates the connections among the author's or illustrator's various works.
- Makes the entire library a potential reading source as children search for more of the author's work and for other books with connecting themes.
- Creates a sense of achievement as readers begin to recognize the connections in the works of different writers and as they identify universal themes and topics.
- Challenges minds to think in new terms as each connection is found between two or more books.
- Brings more books and reading into the curriculum.

Benefits of author programs sponsored by organizations other than schools may be less obvious, but the benefits are there. Organizations that sponsor visits to a public library, art museum, or bookstore benefit students by either including them directly in their plans or by addressing their program to adults who, in turn, will take the enthusiasm back to young readers.

Such was the case in an author visit that was designated as part of a college graduate course for educators. Cynthia Rylant was to speak during the sessions scheduled for a children's literature update class during the summer at a local university. The teachers in this class got to survey Rylant's work and learn about her background and experiences. In her talk, Rylant gave personal insights into her work and answered questions. Many of those who heard her returned to their communities with renewed enthusiasm for sharing Rylant's work with their students. They read her stories aloud, discussed her growing-up years in the Appalachian Mountains and her relationship with her writing, and in general recaptured much of the warm glow they had felt meeting the author in person. Dozens of classrooms benefited even though Cynthia Rylant did not actually visit a school.

Patricia McKissack's appearance at a local children's literature conference had a similar effect. She spoke of her deep commitment to writing stories about African Americans and spoke of her favorite poem, "Little Brown Baby" by Paul Dunbar. She recited a book she had written, *Flossie and the Fox*, and in general inspired those present to read more culturally diverse literature. Teachers came away from that conference committed to using McKissack's books in their curriculum, to sharing some of the enthusiasm she had for bringing good stories to children in storytelling, and to putting drama into language arts activities in their classrooms.

# Getting Organized

This is where the work and fun begin. Now it's time to act on the decisions you've made. Now the focus must turn to establishing the coordinating committee and making the contacts that will result in a successful event. The committee will need to decide who will be invited, what type of event should be planned, and when and where it should be held. It is important that one group oversees the logistics of the entire visit so that there is an overview of the various activities that are occurring. This provides better coordination and gives the publicist, author, or illustrator a single contact for all questions.

## ▷ ESTABLISHING THE COMMITTEE

The composition of the committee depends primarily on the schools, libraries, community organizations, or businesses involved. If an author event involves just one school or one organization, the planning committee formed at that school or organization is responsible for coordinating the visit. If, however, other schools or organizations are cosponsors, each of the sponsoring organizations will need to be represented on the committee.

In one community a local bank significantly underwrites the costs of a weeklong author residency; the bank's corporate vice president serves as an active liaison to the planning committee. Another community has a similar arrangement with corporate sponsorship of an author residency. However, in this instance the financial sponsor prefers to leave the planning to those directly involved and asks only to be advised of the details as they are arranged. In that same community, the area education agency is a joint sponsor, underwriting some of the travel costs, and wishes to be very much involved. So while the coordinating committee is often composed of representatives from each of the sponsoring organizations, its make-up reflects the desires of the individual sponsoring organizations.

Regardless of its composition, the committee is charged with overall coordination of the events as they relate to all of the sponsors and makes decisions that might affect all the participating groups. For example, the group may decide to coordinate the purchase of books for autographing sessions. It would then probably determine the price (retail or discounted) it will charge those who purchase books during the event. The coordinating committee also decides what, if any, other public events to incorporate into the visit. For example, a group planning a large-scale book conference aimed at an adult audience may wish to restrict author visits to nearby schools simply because the educators in those schools would be much less likely to attend the book conference. The committee must weigh how each decision affects the goals for the event.

Once the committee has been formed, the members should begin immediately to make plans and work together to make the proposed visit a reality. They will need to obtain funding and garner official support for the project. Even though they will need to make decisions by consensus, it is important, I believe, to have a committee chair who will assume the overall role of keeping checklists of what has been accomplished, monitoring the expenditures, and so forth. This does not mean that the chair does all the work or makes all the decisions; it merely means that she or he is the overall keeper of the records, chairs meetings, and serves as the contact person. It also means that the chair must have some latitude in making decisions based on the group's general consensus.

This involves latitude in actually selecting an author/illustrator and negotiating for the visit. When talking to the guest artist or his representative, the chair must have a sense of the budget and the overall plan in order to make decisions without going back and forth and wasting everybody's time. The chair will pass on information to the committee members who are responsible for various portions of the visit. Before voice mail and e-mail, this communication involved much telephoning back and forth. At the outset of the planning, members will want to establish committee and subcommittee mailing lists of their e-mail programs.

**TECHNOLOGY TIP!** Those establishing group mailing lists might remember to put those addresses in the "bcc" (blind carbon copy) portion of the e-mail program in order to eliminate those long lists of addresses at the header of every message that is sent.

Early on, the committee should be aware of all the steps in the process and when they should be accomplished. Form 2, "Author/Illustrator Visit: Checklist and Time Line," in Section 8, pages 91-92, will give everyone involved a well-organized overview.

## ▶ FUNDING THE EVENT

One of the committee's first tasks will be to obtain formal support and funding for the proposed visit. Almost two decades ago, children's book publishers began to promote visits as a means of introducing their authors and illustrators and helping them earn supplemental income. The publisher often paid for travel or picked up other expenses in connection with the visit. Over a period of years, the visiting artist idea has caught on with those who work with young readers. The benefits of the visits were so great that the publishers no longer needed to subsidize them. Currently most publishers no longer pay any part of the expenses involved in an author appearance. A few exceptions are made for large conference appearances where the exposure is thought to help both the author's or illustrator's standing in the children's and young adult literature field and public relations in general.

Today, author and illustrator visits are big business. Some artists keep their fees high to discourage invitations that intrude on their creative time. But others promote their speaking engagements and actively seek appearances—and with a high price tag. Some of them charge $2,000 to $5,000 per day, but many are willing to come for honorariums in the range of $400 to $700. (I'll have more to say about honorariums in the next section.)

If committee members have specific authors in mind, it is best to locate some general and biographical information about those artists. For example, one school's committee had their sights set on inviting Paula Danziger, the author of many humorous chapter books, including the Amber Brown series. Danziger is a wonderful presenter, but she spends about half of her year in London, where she is the host of a literary show *Live & Kicking* on BBC, and the rest of the year in New York state. Because of her relatively limited time in America, she appears primarily at larger conferences and conventions.

Committee members will have to decide how much they are willing to spend before they begin to solicit funding. It does not make much sense, I believe, to use an author/illustrator visit in a school to promote reading and then not provide any funds for the library media center to purchase books. It is important to keep everything in perspective. Keep the library media center's annual book budget on the table while you discuss fees for an author/illustrator program. Organizations other than schools may not have the same considerations, but they must keep the total cost in perspective with other events, goals, and objectives.

Funding will usually be a result of official support. The committee's task will involve preparing a presentation to be made to those who may help with the funding. Sometimes this presentation may be informal, as in the case of an administrator who is already committed to the idea. A more formal presentation may be needed in the case of a parent-teacher organization whose experience and background with author and illustrator visits is minimal.

Funding sources may vary according to the type of event the committee decides would be best at this time for their community. Multi-day, multi-host events hold possibilities for multiple sponsors who would share general expenses, such as transportation to the community, promotion, and publicity. Some grant opportunities may specify a cooperative and more global focus than just one community institution.

### PAULA DANZIGER
*The Cat Ate My Gymsuit*
*Amber Brown Sees Red*
*Snail Mail No More*

When Paula Danziger was a college student, she babysat the children of poet John Ciardi.

"He taught me a lot about language. He suggested that I read one of his poems and underline the funny lines in red and the serious lines in blue. At the end you get purple. I try to get that mix—funny and sad. I think that is what people respond to."

— *Paula Danziger*

Purple is her favorite color, and sugar is her favorite "food group." She also likes sushi, ice cream, and pizza with thin crust, extra cheese, capers, olives, and perhaps some sausage. She divides her time between homes in New York and London, where she is the host of a BBC show.

## ▶ HOW MUCH MONEY WILL IT TAKE?

Before any negotiations or contacts with a publicist, author, or illustrator take place, the committee must estimate the costs of the visit and see that it is in balance with estimates of potential funding. Form 3, "Budget Worksheet," in Section 8, page 93 will provide some structure to your calculations.

To estimate the amount of money necessary to fund a visit to your community, obtain a general idea of the possible cost of airline tickets by checking costs for round-trip tickets between your vicinity and each coast. Travelocity's Web site at <http://www.travelocity.com> is an easy-to-use site to check for air transportation costs. Use the higher figure for your budget calculations. Check the cost of hotel and motel accommodations in your area. See if any of them give discounts to nonprofit organizations or for multi-day stays. Be sure to include accommodations for the night prior to the visit and possibly the night after. Add a reasonable allowance to cover ground transportation, meals, and miscellaneous expenses.

Once you've added these expenses together, you can establish the maximum honorarium you will offer the author/illustrator. Generally you will need to pay the honorarium for any day for which

### JACQUELINE BRIGGS MARTIN
*Snowflake Bentley*
*The Lamp, the Ice, and the Boat Called Fish: Based on a True Story*
*Button, Bucket, Sky*

Local authors and illustrators are often overlooked as potential speakers at major conferences or author and illustrator events in their own communities. One year the director of a major children's book conference received a phone call at 6 a.m. the day of the conference, telling her that one of the presenters would not be there because she'd been unable to get out of her local airport the previous evening. The director immediately called on a local author, Jacqueline Briggs Martin. She did not hesitate to agree to speak at the conference. By 10 a.m. she was speaking in front of 300 conference attendees. We learned that day what a truly wonderful resource and friend of literacy we had right in our own community. Her presentation is often remembered as a favorite among those who regularly attend the conference. The moral: Don't overlook inviting *local* artists to be part of your events. The transportation and other expenses will be less, and they have the added advantage of modeling the concept that success can be achieved in your own community. We were all delighted when Martin's book, *Snowflake Bentley*, became the 1999 Caldecott book. More information about her can be found on her Web site at <http://www.jacquelinebriggsmartin.com>.

the author/illustrator will be presenting. Honorariums range from $400 to $1,500.

Sometimes presentations to large groups of adults, such as conference author banquets, require a proportionately larger honorarium. For example, a full day may include three presentations for a $900 honorarium. The same author/illustrator may request a $450 honorarium for a one-hour presentation at a banquet. A few authors, such as Bruce McMillan, establish a per-day fee that includes all travel expenses. The latest information available states that his visits are $1,600 per day and that all visits outside of the New England area must be a minimum of three days. In a case like this, sharing visit arrangements with another school will only help with the three-day requirement—not reduce the cost. Other authors such as Peter Roop, author of *Keep the Lights Burning, Abbie* (Carolrhoda, 1985), quotes his standard speaking fee as a price "per program" with a maximum of four programs per day. That manner of setting an honorarium is gaining in popularity as a means of making clear the limits for any one day's schedule.

Some publishers include information on their Web sites about authors who make school and museum visits or offer "author visit kits." For example, Scholastic makes information about its authors available at <http://teacher.scholastic.com/authorsandbooks/authorvisit/list.htm> and provides suggestions for inviting a Scholastic author to your school or library on its pages at <teacher.scholastic.com/authorsandbooks/authorvisit/index.htm>. Simon and Schuster includes an extensive list of its authors and illustrators, their hometowns and honorariums at its site at <http://www.simonsays.com/>. The Children's Book Council has a site at <http://www.cbcbooks.html.aboutauthors.html> that provides some general information about "Inviting Authors and Illustrators to Your Community" along with links to specific people at various publishing houses to contact about author visits.

Each sponsor will have to agree to the amount of its own financial involvement. Your budget will need to include money for miscellaneous expenses such as phone calls, postage (to confirm details of the visit in writing and send preliminary materials), printing and distribution of publicity, ticket design and printing, promotional activities (author pictures, student book marks in honor of the visit, press releases), film and processing (to record preliminary activities and the events of the actual day), and other unanticipated expenses. While some of these expenses may seem trivial, the total often approaches $100 to $200 per author visit. A planning sheet listing the preliminary budget, an accounting log, and later the statement sheet (Forms 4-6: "Accounting Log,"

"Statement: Expenses and Honoraria," and "Worksheet: Search for Possible Grants or Cosponsors" in Section 8, pages 94-96) should help you keep track of funding and provide important information for future author visits.

The projected total must not exceed expected funding from all sources. You may be able to raise money to help fund the visit by holding an evening event for adults and charging a modest admission fee. In conjunction with such an event, you could hold a book fair featuring the visiting artist's books and other new or popular titles and use the proceeds to help defray expenses for the visit. But since this type of funding cannot be guaranteed, you can't include a set amount in the budget. You *could* count on these fundraisers for additional miscellaneous expenses, such as enrichment activities or producing books children write in conjunction with the visit. You might earmark some of the funds raised outside of the general budget to give a set of the author's or illustrator's books to each sponsoring organization or to lower the cost of books purchased by students. And you could put any excess in a fund for future visits.

When calculating direct costs for the visit, planners often overlook the cost of supplying copies of the guest artist's books for the library media center. You will need to purchase multiple copies, so the cost can quickly add up. If this is a school author event, it is often wise to retain one complete set of books in the library media center so that any child can come into the center to read the books during the day. Also, parents or other interested adults will have them available to preview, especially if the books will be offered for sale to the students and public. A second set of books could be circulated on a reserve basis to teachers, who could use them as read-alouds throughout the author focus period. Additional copies, if you can afford them, can circulate among the students. You can either include the cost for these additional copies in the miscellaneous expenses or list it as a separate item. Once you've completed the budget worksheet, you should have a good idea of the maximum amount you will need.

## ▶ WHERE WILL THE MONEY COME FROM?

Schools and nonprofit organizations often need to look to support organizations for financial help, such as grants for community or educational projects. Usually organizations awarding grants do not become part of the planning committee but provide the financial support in return for some credit and a final report once the event has occurred. The grant-giving organization will generally look at the proposal more favorably if you set forth definite objectives and goals. Seldom does a grant fund the entire cost of the event.

Many states have arts councils or affiliates of the National Endowment for the Humanities that provide grants for events such as author and illustrator visits to schools. Check the National Endowment for the Humanities Web site at <http://www.neh.fed.us/>. There will be a link to state councils that may be helpful. Finding out about organizations that award grants for such events is the key. Contact your state education department to inquire about educational grants that may be available. Links to specific state department of education Web sites are generally available through the appropriate state folder at the 50 States— States and Capitals site, <www.50states.com>. Visit the public library and investigate grant opportunities by perusing the resources that list available grants from the private sector. Scholastic Publishers has a helpful page, "Scholastic—Grants and Funding," on its Web site, <http://teacher.scholastic.com/professional/grants/index.htm>. Several well-written articles by Dr. Gary Carnow are linked from that page along with other helpful pages of information.

With any grant application, be sure to read the criteria and requirements carefully to see if your organization qualifies. Check for deadlines and amount and type of information requested. If a form is required, request it and carefully prepare your grant application to meet every guideline. Send the application in ample time to reach its destination by the deadline. Keep the following questions in mind when preparing your application:

■ Are your goals and objectives clearly stated?
■ Is your time line realistic?
■ Is your actual request clearly stated? Are you

> If you decide to invite a local author/illustrator, partially in consideration of cost, keep in mind that you owe the artist no less in terms of preparedness and promotion than you would give to a higher-priced person from outside your local area.

asking for financial assistance? Printing support? Planning assistance? Discounts on services? Help with promotion?
- Is your application neatly prepared?

One other resource available in many communities is a local author/illustrator who may reduce the honorarium or even make presentations gratis for local schools or nonprofit organizations. Ann McGovern's honorarium is reduced slightly for presentations that don't require an overnight stay. Jean Davies Okimoto is a volunteer writing tutor in the Seattle, Washington "author mentor program" and a creator of the Mayor's Reading Awards for reading improvement in the Seattle public schools. As an extension of her commitment to the reading program, her presentations, for a number of years, have been free for Seattle Public Schools. She also reduces her rates if she is invited to speak in an inner-city school. Another author has simply devoted two presentations a year to be gratis presentations. She selects the groups from among those who have already requested her presentation and bases her choices on her perception of the organization's need, her own charitable interests, and the organization's level of commitment toward literacy in general.

If you should be so lucky as to have a child in your school whose parent or grandparent creates children's books, that person might be willing to visit your school or the child's classroom gratis. Sometimes authors are more willing to visit one classroom at no charge, as opposed to an entire school. Authors and illustrators charge fees because in the children's book market that is one way they can augment their less-than-adequate incomes. Few of them make their entire living from writing children's books. But they are parents and grandparents, and this is one way they could volunteer in your school. If they do agree to come, it is important that the preparations are as intense as if the author were coming from 600 miles away.

Among the first types of organizations often listed as possible donors or sponsors of author and illustrator visits are those that have some direct connections to libraries or schools, for example, "Friends" groups, parent-teacher organizations, or local reading chapters. However, support can often be found within local businesses in your community. Funds for author events have come from community banks, local newspaper foundations, telecommunication companies, and grocery chains. The support may be in the form of actual funds to support the planned events or as in-kind donations. One grocery store offered to print a promotion for a month-long reading program on its grocery bags. It printed 423,000 bags and distributed them over six weeks—a substantial in-kind donation. It also provided refreshments for some community events. In the case of the printed grocery sacks, it was necessary to make connections at least six months in advance. (Moral: Plan early.)

## ▶ A BLUEPRINT FOR A COMMUNITY-WIDE READING INITIATIVE

When an opportunity for an event or promotion presents itself, seize it. The timing may not be of your choosing, but the opportunity is too important to ignore. I will give you an example from my own community, one that had enjoyed several single-day author events, day-long conferences on books for young readers, even author and illustra-

> In addition to obtaining funds from sponsors, consider what other kinds of support you might need, and then consider what person, organization, or company might be willing to donate the item or service—refreshments, printing, advertising, film and photo developing, a floral centerpiece for a dinner, and so forth. Companies often are willing to donate items they sell as their business—florists often donate flowers; grocery stores contribute food; drug stores or photo stores might furnish film or processing.

tor residencies, and was also well known for hosting a very successful annual book conference. However, in recent years, while the author events had continued, the state legislature and the local school board had shifted their priority to providing funds for technology. Public sentiment seemed to be moving in that direction, too. Support was waning for library books, reading, and literacy. This trend had been the topic at several meetings of local school media specialists.

Soon after these informal discussions, the public library was selected to host a major exhibit on mathematics and literature. The exhibit featured interpretive materials on five books with math concepts for two- to seven-year-olds and their parents. Included in the display were scenes from the five books: *Arthur's Pet Business* by Marc Brown, *The Doorbell Rang* by Pat Hutchins, *The Quilt* by Ann Jonas, *Frog and Toad Are Friends* by Arnold Lobel, and *Goldilocks and the Three Bears* illustrated by James Marshall. The math concepts included measuring, sorting, counting, and estimating. The exhibit, sponsored by the American Library Association and several national corporations, was scheduled for six weeks in early spring. As a condition of hosting the exhibit, the library was required to have a public opening, to which library personnel wanted to invite an author. The timing, though, would be close to the community's annual book conference; the two events posed a potential conflict in terms of publicity, audience, and public interest.

The sponsoring organizations decided to capitalize on the appearance of all the authors (three to appear at the book conference and one at the grand opening of the exhibit) by billing the events as part of a larger emphasis on reading and literacy. Thus, the concept for a community-wide focus was born. "Building a Community of Readers" took its name from the national reading report titled "Building a Nation of Readers."

Our first order of business was to gain the support of other community groups. We decided to focus the initiative within a specific metro area that encompassed three cities with a combined population of approximately 150,000, three school districts, three public libraries, five museums and history or science centers, and many civic organizations. When we contacted key personnel at each of the school districts and other institutions and presented the idea of a community-wide reading event, all were immediately interested in being involved. The local area education agency agreed to provide a modest amount of direct financial support but contributed greatly by agreeing to act as fiscal agent.

Our next step was to establish criteria and goals.

**GOALS FOR "BUILDING A COMMUNITY OF READERS" ACTIVITIES:**

- Focus the community on the importance of reading.
- Promote community, school, and family partnerships to improve educational, specifically reading, opportunities for an intergenerational group of learners.
- Provide renewable opportunities for adults to create a positive and literate atmosphere for reading and learning.
- Strengthen intergenerational links to support reading and educational activities in the community.

Since the ALA exhibit focused on mathematics in literature, we were able to contact Loreen Leedy to be the featured author at the exhibit's grand opening. Her many math-themed titles made her a natural choice. Diane Foote, the publicist at Holiday House, graciously helped arrange for Leedy's visit. The local area education agency had teamed with us to help fund two teacher workshops, one to be held the first afternoon of her visit on a day already scheduled as a workshop day for area schools. The grand opening would take place in the early evening. The second workshop, to be held on the following Saturday, would be available to a wider group of teachers in the area. We contacted the mathematics coordinator of one of the larger school districts, and she agreed to fund one-day author residencies in two schools, which allowed us to "hold the author" between the middle of the week workshop and the Saturday morning event. The two schools were selected by lottery.

Other organizations wanting to sponsor an

anchor event were asked to organize and arrange for that event, keeping in mind the goals for each event. A project director did the scheduling to make sure conflicts did not occur. The director also solicited corporate sponsorships for the general expenses and applied for grants from the state Humanities council. Some businesses responded with cash support; others provided in-kind donations. The grant money was earmarked to bring several authors to the community and to promote connections among the organizations.

Anchor events included author residencies and storytelling sessions in ethnic museums and centers, at a historical mansion, and at a private college with the co-sponsorship of the local Catholic schools. Activities included literature sessions at the science station, an official opening message on videotape distributed throughout the community, and invitations for community members to come into the schools to read with the children. In addition to the major ALA exhibit at the largest of the community's public libraries, there were author receptions and signings at the local African-American Historical Museum and Cultural Center, and another author session at the history center. Jane Kurtz, E. B. Lewis, and Eric Kimmel were the featured speakers at a major conference on books for young readers. Other activities included

- A book discussion group—Kava a Kinny (Coffee and Books)—"Stories, Tales, Legends, and Lore," at the National Czech and Slovak Museum and Library,
- A communications network author and illustrator visit with third graders,
- Mathematics-in-literature teacher workshops featuring Leedy, and
- A weeklong Read-a-Thon sponsored by yet another public library.

We chose three authors—Carol Gorman, Craig Brown, and Caroline Arnold—for our author residencies. We were able to pay the transportation costs from the grant and share the honorarium charges.

Literally hundreds of young readers, young adults, parents, and community members of the metro area involved themselves in at least one of the activities. Tabloids promoting the events and activities for parents were distributed throughout the community. Individual schools created their own school-community programs by inviting immediate community members into their school for innovative programs featuring books and connections to readers. All of these activities were conceived and promoted through the core coordinating committee, which tended to generate ideas, help refine suggestions, and assist in implementing the plans.

No one is suggesting that you begin with a multi-event, month-long focus such as this. However, each event is a model in itself of an activity related to an author visit. Each required similar preparation. The moral? Each program or event must be well planned and promoted to the focus audience, and no detail overlooked. The culmination will be a successful literacy event that stimulates reading.

## ▶ IDENTIFYING POSSIBLE COSPONSORS

In addition to seeking grants to fund author and illustrator events, the planning committee can also solicit cosponsors. Organizations that provide grants generally require submission of a proposal, budget, and report at the end of the project but do not participate in the actual planning. Cosponsors usually have a mutual interest in promoting a particular activity or goal. One of the most common arrangements for cosponsors is one involving similar organizations—schools or libraries—each of which will sponsor a day or half-day visit and split the transportation costs and other expenses connected with the visit. Another arrangement might join together the school or library wishing to sponsor an author/illustrator visit with another agency, such as an area education agency or community organization (parent-teacher organization, Jaycees, a business enterprise or bookstore), that would lend financial support as a community service. Sometimes the organization will cosponsor an already planned event. Other cosponsors may wish to have a program at their facility, an evening or Saturday presentation for the community held in conjunction with the school visit, for example.

We have received funds from the local public library's Friends group with the stipulation that our author also present an evening program, open to the public, at the public library. The funds received more than adequately paid for the extra presentation and gave us a broader base for promoting our school events. Another time, the local newspaper supplied funding to help arrange for "readers' workshops" to be held during a day when two authors visited the school. Each talked with groups of students and participated in reading and writing workshops.

Other possible cosponsors include local or state chapters of professional organizations affiliated with the International Reading Association, National Council of the Teachers of English, American Library Association, Children's Literature Association, Society of Children's Book Writers and Illustrators, and others. Often local chapters of these groups invite authors and illustrators as speakers at conferences, programs, and meetings. By scheduling the guest artist's visit to your school or library in conjunction with a visit to an organization's conference or meeting, you may be able to share transportation and other costs. Don't overlook the possibility of collaborating with a local bookstore to host an author event.

A checklist of possible cosponsors may help you ensure that you overlook no candidate. Brainstorm a list of possibilities, then check your list against the checklist in Form 6, "Worksheet: Search for Possible Grants or Cosponsors," in Section 8, page 96. Combine your list and the applicable ideas from Form 6 into one list. In most cases you won't use all the possibilities during any one situation. Because many communities have unique circumstances, there might be a funding source in your area that should be added to the master list. As you check each of the possibilities, be sure to note the name and telephone numbers of the contact person for future use—even if the answer this time is "no."

If you are not interested in pursuing a joint sponsorship arrangement with other organizations, you will want to use the checklist only to search for grants or stipends.

The type of visit your group is interested in arranging will help determine the organizations or groups that you will contact. For example, one year a media association was holding its annual conference in our area. By making contact with the conference committee chair, we were able to dovetail an author visit with her appearance at the conference. In fact, the project grew to include 11 schools that correlated visits with the conference appearance. All shared the transportation costs and each paid a share of the motel, meals, and miscellaneous expenses. Since we were able to offer a multi-day package, the honorarium for each visit was somewhat less than it might have been for a one-day visit.

The only major contact we made that year was to the media association. The schools who wanted to participate were identified through an article in the area education agency's quarterly newspaper. The article solicited schools that wanted to participate by sponsoring a daylong school visit.

Once we identified the interested schools, we formed a coalition of representatives who established the protocol for the entire visit. Representatives from each sponsoring organization were responsible for taking the information and decisions back to their respective schools and helping to establish their own schools' planning and implementation committees.

The coordination of this residency took some time, but one media specialist agreed to take on that task in return for one day of the author's time at her school. She arranged for all the paperwork, hotel reservations, and one honorarium payment. Each school was charged a flat fee that included its share of hotel, meals, and transportation costs and the honorarium. Built into the shares were the expenses for the coordinator's school. The per diem cost was still far below the normal one-day cost for the author's visit. Sometimes, even if you do not wish to be involved in the overall planning, if you are willing to simply be a liaison and book an author into several schools in the area, the author will reduce his fee. If enough schools are involved, he may consent to visit your school for free.

Another year the public library was contacted to sponsor a "conversational meeting" with an author. The area education agency agreed to sponsor an evening event for educators in the area and to give each of the participating schools a modest grant toward the expense of a visit to their schools.

Possibilities for cosponsors may change from year to year, but sometimes a successful event will result in a continuing relationship among the cosponsors. Since 1987, one university community has had a community celebration of reading during the month of November—sponsored, for the most part, by a local bank. The celebration includes an author/illustrator visit. A committee of five media specialists works with a senior vice president of the bank to coordinate the events. In addition to the author visit, the bank funds the printing and distribution of over 10,000 activity calendars emphasizing the reading activities scheduled as part of the reading month activities.

The committee also arranges celebrity read-ins (the bank provides lunch for the readers) and arranges for and promotes storytelling sessions and educational forums for parents and educators. One year, Jim Trelease was invited to speak to parents about the value of reading aloud to children. The visits to schools are scheduled to coincide with a children's and young adults' literature conference at the university. The bank's involvement has become a tradition that emphasizes the cooperative partnership of business and schools as well as the importance of literacy and lifelong learning.

This is a longstanding tradition in that community. As the bank began to grow and establish a presence in other nearby communities, it was difficult to duplicate that same commitment in the new communities. The bank might well have felt it could not afford to support such a program in a second community. So do be creative and attempt to make your request of some "new" sources rather than simply trying to tap into funding sources already established by others.

Once sponsors have been solicited and financial aspects of the visit have been dealt with, it is time to move on to the actual logistics of the visit.

If the sponsors wish to be part of the planning, a representative should be included on the coordinating committee. In most cases, the representative will be the chair or representative from each organization's in-house planning committee. The coordinating committee will be responsible for decisions affecting all participants, while each organization's planning committee will deal with only those decisions that affect that organization. Do elect or appoint a chair of the coordinating committee. Outside agencies, the funding sources, and your school's accounting department all need to know who the point of contact is. That person must have latitude to determine some procedures and make some decisions in line with the established direction of the coordinating committee.

## ▶ INVOLVING COSPONSORS

Ideally, you will have solicited the sponsors and ascertained their level of involvement before the coordinating committee is established. However, as a practical matter, it is often necessary to make arrangements for an author/illustrator visit before some organizations will commit to sponsoring the event. An art museum might be interested in cosponsoring an event featuring an illustrator but may not be inclined to give the same level of support to an author. A public library may wish to sponsor an event that would appeal to young adults but because of other programming commitments would not be interested in sponsoring an event with a picture book author/illustrator.

That was the case described earlier in the "Building a Community of Readers" planning. The public library was hosting the American Library Association's "Go Figure" exhibit, featuring a mathematics and literature connection. They were very much interested in obtaining a featured speaker for the grand opening but were interested only in a speaker who had written books with a strong mathematical connection. They would not have been interested in cosponsoring a visit by an author who did not have such a strong mathematical connection. Once this first connection was made, other organizations were able to make a firm decision based on the specific author who was available.

The first organizations to commit to the concept of sponsoring an author/illustrator event may be considered the "charter" sponsors and may need to make initial arrangements and decisions to enlist additional sponsors. Each of the charter sponsors will seek funding for its share of costs from its own potential benefactors. A school might tap school inservice funds, special funds for student assemblies, or parent-teacher organizations, or might sponsor a fund raiser for the event. Public libraries might have public relations accounts, organizations of friends, or private donors who regularly sponsor this type of event.

If the actual payment of the funds is to come later in the process (or when specific bills are submitted), it is best, at this time, to obtain a written agreement from the sponsoring organizations specifying the amount they are willing to commit. It is not unusual for personnel to change within an organization; one administrator's agreement may not be factored into a new administrator's plans.

Determine if the sponsoring organization will pay specific expenses, for example, air transportation or facility rental, or if the funding will be a set amount. If it is to be a set amount, be sure to specify when the money is to be available. With the obligation in writing, the funding is secured. Once funding is obtained and the sponsors secured, firm commitments can be made with the guest artist.

If there is a potential for additional sponsors, you can pursue the possibility of the artist being available for additional events when you make arrangements with the artist or her publicist. During any discussion of additional events, be careful to present the additional days as possibilities only, ascertain the date that the artist would need to know for sure, and obtain enough information about these possibilities to solicit additional sponsors. It is important to determine what additional honorarium would be required. (In general, each additional sponsor decreases the cost to each sponsor.) As soon as a sponsor agrees to fund a portion of the visiting artist events, the sponsor should be encouraged to nominate a representative to the coordinating committee.

# Making Decisions

## ▶ WHAT TYPE OF VISIT SHOULD YOU PLAN?

"Author/illustrator visit" does not mean the same thing to everyone. Some might define an author/illustrator visit as one day at one school, several days at the same school, or several days in the vicinity with each day spent in a different location. Visits could also be a part of a particular organization's special events, a young authors' day program, a children's literature conference, or author/illustrator gala featuring several authors/illustrators at a celebration of reading and writing.

If you are new to organizing author events, consider making your first experience as simple as possible. You will gain much practical experience and build confidence for more involved arrangements in the future. Whatever type of event you choose to begin with, keep a planning journal in which you record anecdotal notes about the tasks you perform. That journal will prove invaluable as you develop your own style of managing author/illustrator visits.

## *The One-Day, One-Host Event*

Perhaps the most typical author visit is the one-day/one-host event during which an author/illustrator is invited for a one-day or evening visit to your school or library to give a presentation to readers. The one-day visit would be the culmination of an extended focus on the author's/illustrator's books. Other than information sent prior to and thank-you notes sent after the visit, the author's or illustrator's direct involvement is limited to this one day or evening.

## *Young Authors' Day*

A young authors' day focuses on bringing published authors and young writers together to talk about writing. During the months before the author's visit, those who will attend are encouraged to write (and illustrate if they wish) several pieces from which they will select a piece to polish and share in small group sessions at the authors' day. Established writers

### Russell Freedman
*Lincoln: A Photobiography*
*An Indian Winter*
*Eleanor Roosevelt: A Life of Discovery*

During his presentations, Russell Freedman speaks about the research he does in primary sources to gather information for his photobiographies, including his Newbery Award-winning *Lincoln: A Photobiography* (Clarion, 1987). For his book *An Indian Winter* (Holiday, 1992), he traveled to Fort Berthold, North Dakota, where he talked to Mandan Indians. Of the day he spent researching *Lincoln: A Photobiography* in a temperature-controlled vault in the Illinois State Historical Library in Springfield, Freedman said, "I'll never forget that afternoon. . . . There's something magical about being able to lay your hands and eyes on the real thing." The topics of his books have included Indian chiefs, the Wright Brothers, Eleanor Roosevelt, Babe Didrikson Zaharias, and Louis Braille. Freedman also writes of events, such as the writing of the Declaration of Independence in *Give Me Liberty : The Story of the Declaration of Independence* (Holiday, 2000).

help the participants respond to one another's writing in an effort to refine writing skills. In addition, one or more of the guest authors is usually invited to address the student writers at an assembly. Student participants are chosen based on their demonstrated interest in the writing process. Just as budding artists would be selected for special art workshops with an artist, so too are budding writers selected for this type of author visit.

Sometimes the authors' day focuses only on writing, but other authors' days may emphasize procedures related to writing, such as research. Authors, such as biographer Russell Freedman, often emphasize that writing, whether fiction or nonfiction, demands a great deal of research. Freedman begins his research by reading about a subject in the "most relevant books" he can locate. After he reads those sources and creates a bibliography, he does field research. If possible, he interviews people who knew the subject—and he collects photographs. Typically, he selects just 90 to 100 photographs from among a thousand or more that he has collected.

## Children's Literature Festivals and Conferences

Children's literature festivals are another way of bringing authors into your community. Festivals may last several days and typically involve several invited authors in formal presentations, interactive groups, and award banquets. Both children and adults are part of the audiences at these various functions.

A variation on the festival is a children's literature conference. A conference is usually aimed at an adult audience. One successful conference is the Festival of Books for Children and Young Adults, sponsored by the School of Library and Information Sciences at the University of Iowa. This conference has been held each autumn since 1968 in Iowa City. Each year three or four headline guests are invited to come to the campus to present to 300 adult participants. Over the years, the conference has been host to Madeleine L'Engle, Marcia Brown, Gary Paulsen, Lois Lowry, Allen Say, Russell Freedman, Amy Hest, Will Hobbs, Nikki Grimes, and many others.

Another highly successful conference is held in Cedar Rapids, Iowa. The Books Have It... So Do We conference began in 1975. The School Library Association and Encyclopedia Britannica had named the district's library media centers exemplary school media centers, and the media specialists used the prize money to fund an annual children's literature conference. The conference features three notables in the field of children's literature. Usually one guest is an author/illustrator of books for the primary-aged child, a second guest writes for the middle school audience, and a third specializes in using literature in the classroom. The first conference featured Marilyn Sachs, Eric Carle, and Bill Halloran. In subsequent years, guests included

Barbara Corcoran, Arnold Lobel, Beverly Cleary, Katherine Paterson, Leo and Diane Dillon, Ed Emberley, Nicholasa Mohr, Donald Crews, Jacqueline Briggs Martin, James Cross Giblin, Joan Lowery Nixon, David Small, Jane Kurtz, E. B. Lewis, and Eric Kimmel.

## *Multi-Day, Multi-Host Visit*

A variation on a one-day visit is the multi-day, multi-host visit, in which several schools, libraries, or other institutions work together to plan a multi-day visit by the author. In a typical arrangement, each institution hosts an event for one of the days or evenings of the visit. They collaborate on the dates of the visit, but each host is responsible for one day of the visit. It is usually a good idea for one of the host organizations to serve as overall coordinator of the stay, arranging for hotel, transportation, and miscellaneous expenses, and serving as a liaison for the author/illustrator.

The multi-host arrangement offers a great deal of flexibility; the standard author school visit could be the goal of one host institution, while another might wish to ask the author/illustrator to participate in a young authors' day or children's literature festival or to speak to college classes. Of course, each host gets the guest's approval for the type of event it proposes to sponsor.

One multi-day, multi-host visit featuring author/illustrator David Wisniewski included three sponsors—elementary schools, an area education agency (an umbrella agency providing inservice opportunities and support services to several districts within its region), and a public library. During Wisniewski's five-day visit, he spent one day in each of four schools; gave a presentation for parents, students, and educators in the region served by the area education agency; and was involved in a Saturday morning

---

### ALLEN SAY
*Grandfather's Journey*
*Tree of Cranes*
*El Chino*

During a presentation in Iowa City at the annual Festival of Children's Books, Allen Say talked about *Tree of Cranes* (Houghton, 1991), the origins of that story, and the research he conducted in order to write *El Chino* (Houghton, 1990). He also talked about his grandfather, who had immigrated to the United States, married, and later returned to Japan with his wife and child. That child was Allen Say's mother, and the journey became the subject of *Grandfather's Journey* (Houghton, 1993), which won the 1994 Caldecott Award. Say also spoke of his mother's birth in America and her growing-up years in Japan. That story became the basis for *Tea with Milk* (Houghton, 1999).

---

### JANE KURTZ
*Faraway Home*
*The Storyteller's Beads*
*I'm Sorry, Almira Ann*

Jane Kurtz spends many of her days traveling to schools and conferences speaking to children and adults about reading and writing. Her first books came from experiences with her own children. Then she found herself reaching back into her girlhood as a daughter of missionaries in Ethiopia to find the seeds for her early picture books. In her presentations, she speaks of those experiences and how confronting her memories and the knowledge of events that occurred later in Ethiopia led her to write *The Storyteller's Beads* (Harcourt Brace, 1998). In 1997, a flood invaded her family home, an event that led Kurtz to write a series of poems chronicling her emotions and experiences following that flood. Eventually those poems were arranged as a narrative in a book, *River Friendly, River Wild* (Simon & Schuster, 2000). During her presentation, she tells anecdotes from her own and her family's past and tells readers how those stories came to be part of her published books. When Jane visits schools, she often sends artifacts from Ethiopia for the children to explore as they read her books. More information about Jane can be found on her Web page at <http://www.janekurtz.com>.

conversational meeting at the local public library. The library made an effort to include secondary and college students in that meeting as well as members of the general public interested in writing and illustrating children's literature.

Another multi-day, multi-host author visit featured Craig McFarland Brown, who visited 11 schools in 11 days and presented at a Saturday morning brunch during a state media association's spring conference. His visit to the community was funded through a grant by the area education agency, the participating schools, and the state media association.

By paying for the printing, the area education agency benefited because it was able to meet its goal of assisting member schools to promote reading through author/illustrator visits. The state media association benefited since the honorarium for its conference speaker was part of a package that cost less than it would have to contract individually. Each of the schools benefited from this group planning because it would have been much more expensive to arrange for Brown to visit only their school. Each school and organization had a representative on the coordinating committee to share ideas for making the visit a success for everyone involved.

If this is your first encounter with planning for an author/illustrator day, it will be much simpler to focus on just your own organization and not have to consider any other group. However, the costs are usually lower if general expenses can be shared. Some authors/illustrators are willing to lower their per diem rate if given an opportunity to spend more than one day in your general vicinity. Be aware that some authors/illustrators will come for nothing shorter than a two- or three-day visit.

## ▶ WHEN WILL THE EVENT TAKE PLACE?

November (the month of National Children's Book Week), March, and April (the month of National Library Week) are often the months for which authors get the most requests for appearances. For school calendars, these are also the months that allow thorough preparation of the audience. With school starting in late August or early September, there is barely time to adequately prepare for an author visit before November. Then with the interruption of the winter holidays, the next logical time for adequate preparation seems to be March or April. In some northern states, the winter weather is also a consideration.

Because of the popularity of those few months it may be easier to arrange your community's event during another month. If you can do a lot of the preliminary planning and organizing in the spring, you might be ready to begin an author/illustrator focus as soon as school begins in the fall. You could present the author/illustrator unit in the spring and plan the final events for September, just before the author/illustrator's visit. You surely expect the benefits of the author/illustrator visit to endure for a time, so it should be possible to rekindle motivation when school resumes. Our experience has been that once we've made an author/illustrator focus part of our school's activities, the author/illustrator remains a favorite for years. The enthusiasm is relatively simple to revive.

Dates may also be influenced by special events, such as an organization's conference that might provide an opportunity for a cosponsorship. Each member of the coordinating committee should check her own organization for best dates and possible conflicts. Once you put together the information, check other major community organizations.

Find out about availability by talking with the author/illustrator or her publicist. Do not assume that she will spend a full day visiting with children in a school and also be willing (or able) to make a presentation to a group of adults in the evening. Four presentations is the maximum that can be expected for a full-day visit to any school or library. If an evening presentation is to be part of the day's events, schedule fewer presentations during the day. A Web page about Mike Thaler's author appearances sets his honorarium at $1,500-plus and indicates he will give only two presentations a day. If I were planning a Thaler visit, I would plan for adequate space and make sure that his presentation was appropriate for a large group of students. Showing slides allows all to see the visuals, but holding up a picture book in front of an audience of 100 children won't work.

Sometimes sponsoring organizations feel that they must get the "most for their money" and wish to schedule the entire day, squeezing in six or more sessions. The fact is that once an audience exceeds 70, it does not make a lot of difference how much larger it becomes if the available space can accommodate that number of people. Thus, fewer sessions presented to larger audiences will allow the guest author/illustrator to be more relaxed and to have time to interact with students in autographing sessions, informal chats, or visits to classrooms.

Bruce McMillan, a writer and photo-illustrator, includes a typical schedule for one of his visits in a brochure he sends in response to inquiries. He suggests a 45-minute session with kindergarten through second grade and a second session of 60 minutes with third- through sixth-grade students. After lunch with the staff, he visits classrooms to answer questions. Later in the day, he presides at an afternoon assembly where he shows a 30-minute film about his work. At the end of the day, he autographs books. He is willing to speak to parents and children or adult groups at an evening presentation, but there is an added fee.

Authors/illustrators Johanna Hurwitz, Gordon Korman, Steven Kroll, Betsy and Giulio Maestro, Louis Sachar, Gary Soto, and Susan Beth Pfeffer all indicate that three presentations a day is their maximum, while Hans Wilhelm and Ann McGovern limit their presentations to two per day. John Peterson, creator of the series about the Littles, prefers to make one large presentation, "How I Write Books and How They are Published," during which he shows slides and often does some drawings. Later he will visit classrooms. The number of

## LOUIS SACHAR
*Sideways Stories from Wayside School*
*There's a Boy in the Girls' Bathroom*
*Dogs Don't Tell Jokes*

Louis Sachar studied to become a lawyer, but the final year of his college work was also the year his first novel was accepted for publication. That title, *Sideways Stories from Wayside School* (Follett, 1978; Avon, 1985) did not bring him immediate success but encouraged him enough that he eventually decided he would rather write than wear a suit and appear in court. He received a lot of letters from children; one class of children in Plano, Texas, wrote several times to ask him to visit their classroom. They were playing cupid for their single teacher. One day while visiting Dallas, Sachar did visit their school. He liked the teacher, but it was the counselor, Carla Askew, who interested him most. In 1985 they were married, and eventually the couple settled in Austin, Texas, where they now live with their daughter Sherre.

Sachar wrote his novel *Holes* (Farrar Straus & Giroux, 1998), which went on to win the prestigious Newbery Award (1999), after an aborted attempt to write a book for adults. He says he "enjoys writing for children" but learned to write for them by reading books written for adults. "I like the short and jumpy opening chapters and how they lead into the story."

presentations will be a factor in determining the number of days that each organization may wish to have the author/illustrator.

Some authors/illustrators, such as Suzy Kline, are available only during the summer or public-school breaks. Others, such as Paul O. Zelinsky and Susan Terkel, will not travel on Jewish holidays. Marilyn Sachs will travel only one day from her San Francisco home, and Barthe DeClements prefers the West Coast. Information like this is important when it comes to choosing a date for an author/illustrator visit.

## Choosing a Date

Poll your cosponsors to ascertain the needs of each and then decide on the schedule for the author/illustrator visit. The schedule you develop at this time should be concerned only with what event will take place first and, if there is to be an evening or weekend presentation, when that event will take place. This is necessary because sometimes a date is a conflict for one of the visi-

### PAUL O. ZELINSKY
*Rumpelstiltskin*
*Hansel and Gretel*
*The Wheels on the Bus*

Paul O. Zelinsky grew up in the Chicago area, attended Yale University, and now lives in New York with his family. One day, before he began his career in children's books, he and a friend were driving through Connecticut when the friend commented that Robert Lawson lived nearby. Momentarily, Zelinsky was astonished. One of his favorite authors was a real person and lived in this real world. Now Zelinsky is part of that world. His oil paintings somberly illustrate the forest settings and menacing interior of the woodcutter's house in Rika Lesser's retelling of Grimm's *Hansel and Gretel* (Dodd, 1984). His illustrated versions of *Rumpelstiltskin* (Dutton, 1986) and *The Wheels on the Bus* (Dutton, 1990) earned him Caldecott Honor Awards in 1987 and 1991. In 1997, Dutton Children's Books published *Rapunzel*, and again Zelinsky was given the 1998 Caldecott Award for the illustrations in that book.

He enjoys learning about the stories he illustrates. Once he establishes a setting for his retellings, he researches the details in his effort to make his illustrations authentic. For example, when he began the illustrations for *Rapunzel,* he decided the story would be set in Italy in 1500. Thus, when he put Rapunzel's hand-mirror in an illustration, he knew it would have to be silvered, convex glass since mirrored flat glass was not produced in Italy before the 1530s. He also decided what the height of the tower and other buildings would be so that he could keep the other figures in proportion to those heights.

tation sites but not for the others. Each sponsor's in-house planning committee can develop the schedules for its school or library.

Survey the master calendars of each organization involved in the visit and pick appropriate dates and at least two alternative sets of dates. Check on school calendars for inservice or conference days and holidays. If any of the author events is to be open to the public, the committee will want to list the dates of other community-wide events that might compete with the author/illustrator visit. If, for instance, you are going to include a night event for parents and educators, it's important not to schedule it on the same night as the PTA award banquet or a reading association's mini-conference.

Appoint a member of the committee to contact those organizations for possible conflicts. It may be helpful to use a form (see Form 7, "Worksheet: Tentative Dates for the Author/Illustrator Visit," in Section 8, page 97) to record this information. In addition to checking for conflicts, by calling you are also alerting the other organizations that you are planning an event so they may make an effort to avoid that date in their own planning.

Once you've checked for conflicts, use the information in contacts with publishers or the authors/illustrators. Any conflicts you identify need not eliminate a set of dates, but you will need to weigh their importance to your prospective audience. If the local college is presenting its third performance of a play on the same evening you hoped to schedule an event for parents, weigh the effect the play may have on attendance at your event. You may decide in favor of going ahead and scheduling the event on your preferred date despite the play. However, if three nearby elementary schools have scheduled open houses for parents and children during the same week you would like to schedule an evening event for elementary parents, you might do best to settle on an alternative date. Those are decisions you will have to make in conjunction with the publicist or the author/illustrator.

## ▶ CHOOSING AN AUTHOR/ILLUSTRATOR

The first consideration for the selection of an author/illustrator is the intended audience or audiences. If the audience is kindergartners to sixth graders, the author/illustrator will have to have some appeal to a range of ages. Often it is easier to adapt activities involving picture books (either fiction or informational) to a group of older students than to adapt activities involving a novel or text-filled nonfiction book to younger students. Obviously the narrower the age or grade range, the easier it will be to choose an appropriate author/illustrator.

Even in schools that emphasize literature and knowledge about authors and illustrators, children often do not have a concept of the relative fame of specific artists.

In our school, the books of Craig McFarland Brown and Carol Gorman are just as popular as those by Steven Kellogg or Tomie dePaola. Children in our school enjoy meeting either one of them as much as they would enjoy meeting Kellogg or dePaola. Much of this is due to teachers' efforts to make Gorman and Brown celebrated authors/illustrators in our school community. Although "selling" Kellogg's and dePaola's books may take less effort (especially with adults, who are probably already familiar with their work) and there are certainly more commercial materials focusing on dePaola and Kellogg, the expense of inviting either of them to your community would be far greater than inviting someone such as Gorman or Brown. Both Kellogg and dePaola are booked over 18 months in advance; their honoraria are well above $1,000. Gorman and Brown are not scheduled so far in advance and are available for a significantly lower honorarium.

Adults are aware of the relative popularity of each of these authors/illustrators, but that popularity is often more important to them than it is to the children.

### CAROL GORMAN
*Jennifer-the-Jerk Is Missing*
*The Miraculous Makeover of Lizard Flanagan*
*Dork in Disguise*
*Dork on the Run*

Carol Gorman became a writer at the urging of her writer husband. After several years of teaching part-time and writing part-time, Gorman became a full-time writer. She does extensive research to establish the background for her books. When she wrote *Dork in Disguise* (HarperCollins, 1999), she read many science articles and talked to high school science teachers. Incorporated into her book was accurate information about building a hovercraft and other scientific subjects.

When she visits schools, Gorman brings with her an infectious love of writing. She talks about how she began writing and describes a typical writing day. She shows students an original manuscript and shares how a book evolves from idea to publication. Her presentation emphasizes the importance of revision in the writing process; she offers students suggestions on how to improve their own writing and where they can submit their work for publication. She often brings a 16" x 20" photograph of the original cover painting for one of her books and discusses why the illustration is effective in selling the book. Several of her books have been awardwinners. More about Carol Gorman can be found on her Web site at <http://www.geocities.com/carolgorman_2000>.

### TOMIE dePAOLA
*Strega Nona Takes a Vacation*
*26 Fairmont Avenue*
*Here We All Are*

Tomie dePaola has illustrated more than 200 books. Among his most popular picture books are those about Strega Nona. In 1999, one of his first autobiographical chapter books, *26 Fairmont Avenue*, was published by G.P. Putnam. It earned dePaola a 2000 Newbery Honor Award and was the beginning of the 26 Fairmont Avenue series. Extremely popular, dePaola receives about 100,000 fan letters a year. He seldom visits individual schools but does make himself available for conference appearances, where he commands an honorarium of more than $1,000 and is booked two years in advance. His full schedule of activities is often listed on his Web site at <http://www.tomiedepaola.com>.

## JON SCIESZKA AND LANE SMITH
*The True Story of the 3 Little Pigs! by A. Wolf*
*The Stinky Cheese Man*
*Math Curse*
*Time Warp Trio Series*

Jon Scieszka and Lane Smith are among those who can ask for large honorariums and are booked well in advance. Scieszka has a two-year waiting list. Their popularity increased considerably with the publication of *The True Story of the 3 Little Pigs! by A. Wolf* (Viking, 1989). In addition to the Time Warp Trio books and *The True Story of the 3 Little Pigs! by A. Wolf*, Scieszka and Smith have collaborated on *The Stinky Cheese Man and Other Fairly Stupid Tales* (Viking, 1992). Another of Scieszka's popular titles, *The Frog Prince, Continued* (Viking, 1991), was illustrated by Steven Johnson. It was Scieszka's wife, Jeri Hansen, who introduced him to Lane Smith and his wife Molly Leach. Scieszka, Hansen, and their daughter, Casey, and son, Jake, live in the Park Slope section of Brooklyn, New York. Smith and his wife live nearby. More about the two book creators can be found on their Web site at <http://www.chucklebait.com>.

## CRAIG MCFARLAND BROWN
*Barn Raising*
*Tractor*
*In the Spring*

Craig McFarland Brown talks to children about dreams as "something you can go back to later," and he talks about his own work as part of the dream he went back to. He bolsters his audience's perceptions of themselves by telling them that they, too, can dream, and that if they really want that dream, it will come to them with patience and work. His books are often set in the Midwest where he grew up in Iowa farm country. When he wrote of an Amish barn raising, he returned to his roots to research images in the Amish community in Kalona, Iowa. When he needed to research a book about raisins by Pam Muñoz Ryan, he had to go west to grape country. More information about Craig Brown may be found on his Web site at <http://www.geocities.com/craigbrown_2000>.

Meeting a "real" author/illustrator will be the memorable element for most students. Thus, when you and your committee begin to choose an author/illustrator, discuss first of all his appeal to the age levels targeted for the visit. Sometimes a publicist will suggest an author/illustrator who will be just right for your goals and objectives.

Craig McFarland Brown was relatively unknown to us when a mutual friend, a publishing house editor, suggested that he might be someone we would be interested in for a visit to our school. We were charmed by his beautiful illustrations, his stories, and the possibilities for extending his books from kindergarten to fifth grade by using them for theme-related activities. The coordinating committee decided to invite him, and no other author/illustrator could have enthralled the students more than he did.

The first year I was at one school, virtually the only two authors the children knew were Dr. Seuss and Beverly Cleary. If we had depended on inviting only authors that the children knew and already enjoyed, those two would have been the only options. And since Dr. Seuss was no longer living and Beverly Cleary was no longer making school visits, we would have had no choice. Part of the purpose of an author visit, I think, is to extend the audience's knowledge of and familiarity with literature and the people who create it.

After that first visit, which was immeasurably successful, the boys and girls in the school repeatedly spoke of Brown as their genuine friend. They often referred to him with a phrase such as "When Craig Brown was here . . . ." In fact, children who began attending our school in later years began to think of him as their friend too. Eventually we invited Brown back so that the younger children could meet him in person, even though many of them felt they had already met him. He became a legend of sorts at our school.

## Creating an Environment for Participation

Depending on the specific author/illustrator you invite, you will want to create an environment that will allow the visit to be meaningful to a wide range of participants. Picture books can be used in the intermediate or middle school classrooms, and novels can be read aloud in the primary classrooms. As you consider whom to invite, brainstorm steps you could take to stretch her appeal down into the primary or upward to the upper-intermediate or middle grades. If your committee is thinking about asking a creator of picture books to speak with older students, consider some of the following possibilities for activities that will help to acquaint them with the artist and her books.

### CYNTHIA LEITICH SMITH
*Jingle Dancer*
*Rain Is Not My Indian Name*

Cynthia Leitich Smith's first picture book, *Jingle Dancer* (Morrow/HarperCollins, 2000), tells a contemporary story about a young Muscogee (Creek)-Ojibwa (Chippewa) girl who longs for a jingle dress of her own. By borrowing on the tradition of the women in her family, she is able to bring together the regalia she needs to dance in a jingle dress. The story takes place in an intertribal Native American Indian community in small-town Oklahoma.

Smith's second book is a novel, *Rain Is Not My Indian Name* (HarperCollins, 2001), which has a young woman attempting to deal with the loss of her friend and her own struggle with her identity.

Cynthia Leitich Smith is of "mixed blood" and is an enrolled member of the Muscogee-Creek. She lives with her husband Greg and their two tabby cats in Austin, Texas. Visit her Web site at <http://www.cynthialeitichsmith.com>.

- Focusing on writing and illustrating as a career opportunity. An author/illustrator such as Craig Brown speaks of returning to a dream—a dream he's held since childhood. Such authors as Jerry Pinkney, James Ransome, E. B. Lewis, Cynthia Leitich Smith, Allen Say, and Tololwa Mollel can provide minority role models.

- Studying the illustrator's artistic technique. Illustrators such as Eric Carle and Gerald McDermott use collage. Leo and Diane Dillon use various techniques, including watercolor, acrylic, pastels, tempera, and sepia, and many tools, including cotton, airbrushes, and conventional brushes. Patricia Polacco uses Pentel markers, acrylic paint, numbers 2B and 6B pencils, and oil pastel. Some artists use batik (Mildred Peck Taylor), stippling (Craig Brown), scratchboard (Brian Pinkney), cut-paper collage (David Wisniewski), and oil paintings (Thomas Locker). Others use various techniques, such as chalk or pen and ink.

- Studying the author's/illustrator's life and the elements of his work that reflect his background. Learning about an author's/illustrator's background helps students use incidents in their own or their friends' lives as the basis for writing and illustrating their own stories. Craig Brown's many books reflect his rural Iowa background. Robert Quackenbush gathered many of his story ideas from his then young son Piet's experiences. Gerald McDermott admired the work of Joseph Campbell and drew many of his motifs and images from the myths and folklore he came to know through his study of Campbell's work.

- Reading the picture books to readers at lower grade or age levels. Develop collaborative reading lists to help those students focus on a theme related to the author's/illustrator's books. For example, while focusing on Craig Brown's books, you might extend the reading to other books with a farm theme. However, be careful to continue to emphasize which ones are those written by the featured author. One way to do that is to have the featured author's books on display on a bookshelf in

## GERALD MCDERMOTT
*Anansi the Spider*
*The Stonecutter*
*Papagayo*
*Musicians of the Sun*

Gerald McDermott lives in Southern California. The Caldecott Medal winner for *Arrow to the Sun* (Viking, 1974) prefers to appear at conferences. He speaks of his respect for folklorist Joseph Campbell and of the motifs and images that are contained in myths and folklore. First as a filmmaker, he retold folktales in that medium and only later adapted each story into a picture book format. His stories come from many cultures: *Arrow to the Sun* is a story from the Pueblo Indians; then there is *Stonecutter: A Japanese Tale* (Viking, 1973). *Anansi the Spider* (Holt, 1972), *The Magic Tree* (Holt, 1973), and *Zomo the Rabbit* (Harcourt, 1992) are all tales from various parts of Africa. McDermott has also told stories from Ireland and Egypt and from Roman mythology. *Musicians in the Sun* (Simon & Schuster, 1997) was created from a fragment of an Aztec tale. He creates many of his book illustrations with collage, others with paintings. McDermott now works as the Primary Education Program Director for the Joseph Campbell Foundation on Mythology in Education. More about the project and McDermott's role as director can be found on the World Wide Web at <http://www.jcf.org/>.

## STEVEN KELLOGG
*Pinkerton, Behave!*
*A Penguin Pup for Pinkerton*
*Best Friends*
*Paul Bunyan*

Steven Kellogg speaks to groups of all ages. He generally talks for a few minutes about his work and then sketches while he retells the story he says is his favorite, *The Island of the Skog* (Dial, 1977). He leaves the sketches for those attending the presentation. He works in a studio in his 200-year-old home in the Connecticut countryside. His Pinkerton books, in the beginning, were inspired by the family's harlequin Great Dane. Eventually a cat, Second-Hand Rose, came into the family and added more inspiration. During some conferences, Kellogg has departed from his usual presentation to speak of the dogs (and sometimes "hogs") in his life.

the library or classroom so that the visual images are those the children remember. Refer to that shelf frequently and never place one of the collaborative reading books on that shelf.

- Locating and reading novels that have a theme similar to that contained in the picture book by the author/illustrator who will visit. Compare and contrast the thematic elements in each of the books. For example, Steven Kellogg's book *Best Friends* (Dial, 1987) focuses on the theme of friendship—a common theme in many early reading books and novels—so crossing over from the picture book to novel should not be difficult. Eileen Christelow's *Jerome the Babysitter (Clarion, 1985)* is a picture book that focuses on problems involved with a babysitting job—a topic also present in several novels by Willo Davis Roberts. Jacqueline Briggs Martin's Caldecott title *Snowflake Bentley* (Houghton Mifflin, 1998) makes a great biography with which to begin a focus on people who dream dreams and persist in reaching their goals. The story can inspire readers to search out biographies of other interesting people, of inventors, explorers, and political figures—anyone who has led an interesting life. Writers might be motivated to write an account of their own lives or the life of someone in their family whom they admire. Many other authors have written books that motivate writing and more reading. Depending on which picture book author/illustrator is to be invited, you may find novels by other authors that can be used as part of critical reading activities.

- Writing or illustrating a book patterned on a type of picture book. For example, Jerry Pallotta has written many alphabet books about specific groups of animals or plants. His icky bug book moves alphabetically through information about icky bugs. His furry animal book deals with information about mammals whose names are listed alphabetically. Gail Gibbons writes many nonfiction books about events or places that exist around her. She visited a skyscraper building site when she wrote *Up Goes the Skyscraper!* (Four Winds, 1986), and she spent many hours at a pottery as she was writing *The Pottery Place* (Harcourt, 1987). Using her books as models for research could provide some interesting activities for older students, as could writing information-packed alphabet books such as Jerry Pallotta's.

If you are thinking about inviting an author of novels to visit with younger students, consider some of the following suggestions:

- Authors who write for a variety of age levels. For example, Steven Kroll, Helen V. Griffith, Cynthia Rylant, Nancy Willard, Judy Delton, and Eve Bunting all write picture books or early reading books as well as novels. Eve Bunting often deals with controversial topics. In *The Wall* (Clarion, 1990), she dealt with the memories of the Vietnam War; in *Smoky Night* (Harcourt, 1994), she dealt with the riots in the Watts area of Los Angeles, and in *Fly Away Home* (Clarion, 1991), the topic was the homeless. Her book *The Memory String* (Clarion, 2000) deals with a young girl's loss of her mother and her efforts to deal with that loss. *Ducky* (Clarion, 1997) is a story inspired by an accidental dumping of a crate of rubber ducks into the Pacific Ocean. Her intermediate-grade and young adult novels have dealt with universal concerns, and sometimes controversial topics, while appealing to older readers.

- Authors whose novels can be read aloud to a younger audience and then extended with thematic books to other reading levels.

- Authors who write picture-filled informational books that might be shared visually with

---

### JERRY PALLOTTA
*The Furry Alphabet Book*
*The Bird Alphabet Book*
*The Icky Bug Counting Book*

"When I write books, I write them the way I would talk to a kid. I ask myself what kinds of things would interest kids. Sometimes I select plants or animals because of their exotic or silly names and other times because of the way they look or behave. I do a lot of research to find out information."
— Jerry Pallotta

### EVE BUNTING
*The Wall*
*The Memory String*
*Fly Away Home*
*Ducky*
*Smoky Night*

Eve Bunting travels from her home in California to make appearances at large conferences and conventions. "Much of my background in Ireland finds its way into my books as does a certain amount of Irish phrasing and Irish philosophy. My children, too, have played large parts, most of the times unwittingly as I lived around them and watched. My writing reflects my concepts and personality. When I'm not writing, which isn't too often as I write every day I am at home, I love to read. There is nothing better than a sunny beach, a comfortable deck chair, and a good book, except a rainy night, a warm fire, and a good book."
— Eve Bunting

### JIM AYLESWORTH
*Old Black Fly*
*The Gingerbread Man*
*The Tale of Tricky Fox*

Jim Aylesworth began his writing career while he was teaching first graders in Hinsdale, Illinois. He read—and sometimes sang—some of his first manuscripts to his students, all the while piling up rejection slips. Eventually, though, he was offered a book contract. Now he often travels around the country speaking at schools about his books. Among his most popular is *Old Black Fly* (Holt, 1992), in which the refrain is "Shoo Fly Shoo." During one visit to a school in Florida, he showed off his "Shoo Fly 'Shoe'"—a clever play on the phrase. When Aylesworth speaks to audiences, he emphasizes being persistent in one's efforts to reach a goal and displays the stack of rejection slips that he has collected on the way to reaching his goal of becoming a published author. His books are filled with rhyme and rhythm and sometimes have a food connection. The back jacket of *The Tale of Tricky Fox* (Atheneum, 2001) includes a recipe for "Eat-Your-Hat" cookies. Of course, the connection between *The Gingerbread Man* (Scholastic, 1998) and gingerbread cookies is obvious.

younger readers. For example, Russell Freedman's *Lincoln: A Photobiography* and *The Wright Brothers* (Holiday House, 1991) feature photographs that can be used with younger children while discussing the subject. The children can then read other books about Abraham Lincoln or Orville and Wilbur Wright.

■ Authors, such as Carol Gorman, who write mainly for an intermediate or middle-school audience. You can read selected novels by Gorman aloud to groups as young as first grade. *Jennifer-the-Jerk Is Missing* (Simon & Schuster, 1994), *Dork in Disguise* (HarperCollins, 1999), and its sequel, *Dork on the Run* (HarperCollins, 2001), are examples of novels that will make first to fourth graders as well as older students laugh.

Add other ideas generated by committee members and decide what approaches would be appropriate for the audiences they represent. Public libraries will have different needs from school libraries. A public library may schedule a special author session on a Saturday for young readers and offer a four-session "workshop" the preceding Saturdays in conjunction with that visit, during which the children can hear and enjoy the author's books read aloud. In such a situation, some of the activities used in the school library media center might be used in the public library's workshop sessions. Or the public library could sponsor a workshop for adults, who would share some of the information and activities with young readers before the author's/illustrator's appearance.

## Making a List of Possibilities

Several publishing houses, such as Scholastic, Inc. and Putnam USA, provide author/illustrator appearance kits that list artists who are available for visits. Give the publisher the opportunity to be involved in your planning as early in the process as possible. The publishing house contact, usually a publicist or marketing director, will be able to provide useful guidance and information. Publishing houses can provide general information about author visits, and once you have decided whom to invite, specific information as well.

Brainstorm a list of authors/illustrators who might fit into the approaches you have chosen, but be flexible. One committee brainstormed a list that began with Beverly Cleary (no longer makes school appearances), Joan Carris (lived in England at the time, making transportation costs prohibitive), Jan Brett (honorarium much higher than the committee's $750 per day budget), Paul Galdone (no longer living), Eric Carle (no longer makes school visits), Gail Gibbons (honorarium over $1,000 per day), Cynthia Rylant (prefers not to travel), Stephen Gammell (refuses most speaking requests), and Bill Peet (no longer speaks to groups of any type because of throat cancer).

Authors/illustrators often have preferences and needs that will affect your decisions. Gerald McDermott prefers conferences, but Natalie Kinsey-Warnock will speak only to children's groups. Amy Ehrlich will make author visits in her local area (Vermont) or at large conferences. Others travel only on weekends or in their home states, but many travel almost anywhere, at any time. This is where the publishing house contact will be able to help immensely.

The publicist's lists will be helpful, but there are many author's/illustrators whose names will not appear on lists—often because their publisher does not have a list or they publish with a variety of publishers and no one publisher is responsible for the promotion of their books. It is important the committee articulate objectives for the visit and give the liaison person authority to make tentative arrangements (subject to final approval) for alternative authors/illustrators who might fulfill those objectives.

Some publisher's kits indicate the amount of each author's/illustrator's honorarium. Some carefully state that negotiations may be possible. In the middle 1990s, a survey conducted for the Society of Children's Book Writers and Illustrators (*SCBWI Bulletin*, Dec. 1993/Jan. 1994, p. 4) indicated that the average honorarium was $550 and often ranged between $200 and $1,500. Ten years later, it would be very rare to find an author or illustrator willing to make an appearance for $200, but many will still consider a visit in the $600-$800 range.

Sometimes local authors will significantly reduce their standard honorarium since there is little travel time. There is quite a difference if an author must prepare a speech, then spend an entire day traveling to a location, present a third day, then spend another day going home—more than three days away from the author's writing schedule. A local author might be able to cut two days from that time if she can travel to the site the morning of the visit. Of course, the presentation time remains the same.

---

### ARNOLD ADOFF
*Hard to Be Six*
*In for Winter, Out for Spring*
*Love Letters*

In response to a written request for an interview, Arnold Adoff sent a short reply asking that he be called on the telephone to arrange for a convenient time to talk. That phone call led to a brief conversation in which we established a time two days later when Adoff would be available for a more lengthy conversation. The second call yielded all the information we needed. While the talk was mostly about his poetry, I found it interesting that Adoff does not have a driver's license, so he doesn't drive, and when his wife, Virginia Hamilton, turns on her computer he would rather back away. In fact, he says he still likes his Smith Corona. Hamilton has a Web site at <http://www.virginiahamilton.com>

---

Other considerations might involve the possibility of a multi-day visit, which makes more efficient use of travel time so that the author might agree to a lower per diem fee. The HarperChildren's Web site actually suggests that if you live in an exotic place, such as Hawaii, the author might agree to negotiate the honorarium in return for a tour of the location or simply for the opportunity to go there. For example, after 25 years of visiting schools, Jane Yolen no longer speaks in schools but maintains an active schedule of book signings and conference appearances. She is particularly receptive to conference invitations in areas where her children reside. She is very willing to participate in conference calls or online chats with students. She can be reached at <janeyolen@aol.com>, and more information about her can be located on her Web site at <http://www.janeyolen.com>.

"Books About Author/Illustrators" in Section 9, page 114-115 will help you research your prospective guests and decide whether or not to keep them on the list. This book also contains a list of "Author/Illustrator Web Sites" in Section 9. Several publishers maintain Web sites with information about the authors/illustrators whose books they publish. In addition, the marketing director or publicist at each of the publishing houses will have some of the same information, often in prepared packets. A good link to those publishers' Web sites is David

K. Brown's Children's Literature Guide at <http://www.ucalgary.ca/~dkbrown/index.html>. The page with the links to publishers' pages can be accessed directly at <http://www.ucalgary.ca/~dkbrown/publish.html>. Another general site leading to publisher sites is the Children's Book Council site at <http://www.cbcbooks.org>. Click on the "members" link.

Once you've generated your final list and discussed the possibilities for using an author's illustrator's work in the classroom, the committee's liaison should begin to make contacts that will result in arrangements for the visit.

## *Extending the Invitation*

It is impossible to list precise steps to take to arrange for an author/illustrator to visit your community because each artist and each publishing house works in a slightly different way. Some authors/illustrators prefer that their publishing house publicist be contacted while others book their own appearances. Some publishing houses prefer to have all requests in writing; others prefer a phone call with a follow-up letter. The HarperCollins' children's site at <http://www.harperchildrens.com> states that that house prefers invitations to come by phone or e-mail rather than by letter.

Usually the best place to begin is to contact the publishing house that publishes your first-choice author/illustrator and ask for the "author appearance coordinator" for the young readers' division. I prefer to call the publisher to inquire to whom the letter should be addressed or if the publisher's representative prefers the inquiry to come via e-mail. The cost of the telephone call is minimal, and it prevents the letter or e-mail from being misdirected at the publishing house. The call can also confirm the current postal mailing address or the appropriate e-mail address. If, however, you do not wish to call and you don't know the name of the coordinator, address the envelope to the publishing house to the attention of "young reader author appearance coordinator." Sometimes the e-mail address of the appropriate contact person can be located on the publisher's Web site.

The addresses of major publishers, most of them members of the Children's Book Council, Inc., are listed in Section 9. However, it is difficult to keep up with the changes in ownership, publishing groups, imprints, and current addresses, and reference works are out-of-date in regard to publishing house addresses sometimes even before they are published. Many publishers are being swallowed up by other publishers. For example, a long-time publisher, Morrow, was purchased by HarperCollins Publishing, and all of Morrow's imprints were discontinued except for the Greenwillow imprint. Telephone calls will save you time waiting for responses to letters sent to outdated addresses. I often check the current advertisements in professional journals for the most up-to-date addresses of specific publishing houses. The publisher's Web sites can also provide up-to-date information. At one time I would have recommended checking *Books in Print* and *Literary Market Place* for publishers' addresses, but those volumes cost so much that I do not keep them in either my home office or library media center office. Currently, in my opinion, the availability of the information on the World Wide Web makes those sources obsolete for the purpose of locating publisher address.

Make sure you have all needed information on hand before you begin making phone calls. The "Worksheet: Author/Illustrator Appearance" (Form 8 in Section 8, page 98) may help you get your information organized. Sometimes even if you merely intend to inquire about the name and address, the operator may connect you immediately to the publicist or author appearance coordinator. Always make complete notes of all conversations.

When you telephone, be prepared to discuss
- Whom you want to invite; provide alternatives if possible.
- When you want the author/illustrator to appear. (Six months in advance is the minimum time recommended.)
- The amount of the honorarium you are prepared to offer and details concerning the other expenses your organization will cover.

- Specifically where in the community the author/illustrator will be speaking.
- Expectations for the author's/illustrator's appearance—formal presentation, question-and-answer sessions, autographing sessions—as well as to whom the artist will be speaking—young children, intermediate students, teenagers, adults, general public, educators—and the approximate number of people in the audience.

If you do decide to phone the publicist before writing, try, if possible, to speak directly with the publicist. If not, be sure to note the name of any assistant you speak with. Explain the committee's total proposal and determine what the role of this specific publicity department will be. The single best help in arranging an author/illustrator visit is a helpful publicist at the appropriate publishing house.

Sometimes the publicist will have alternative suggestions for an author/illustrator who may fit your group's criteria. The author/illustrator you request may have an honorarium far above your projected budget. The publicist will know rates and general availability of specific authors/illustrators. He may be able to suggest authors/illustrators whose rates do fit your budget. He will also be able to tell you if the author/illustrator prefers to make her own arrangements.

Whether you make the first contact by phone, letter, or e-mail, it may take several weeks to arrange for a specific author's/illustrator's visit and there still won't be any guarantees that your efforts will be successful. For that reason, if you have various authors/illustrators in mind, contact several publicists and let each know that you are pursuing other suggestions as well. If you are able to reach an author/illustrator directly, coming to an agreement is much speedier.

Once you have made a firm commitment with an author/illustrator or publicist, let others you have contacted know promptly that you have made arrangements. I personally prefer to identify an author/illustrator that the committee wishes to invite, call the publicist, explain the total proposal, and then if the requested author/illustrator is not available, rely on the publicist to identify others who might fit into the total plan. If this does not work out for some reason, then I proceed to another choice on our list.

This situation occurred when the public library asked my help in obtaining an author to accompany its mathematics and literature exhibit. Among the choices of authors we brainstormed were Stuart Murphy and David Schwartz. A call directly to Murphy—I had his card from meeting him at a reading conference—let me know that he was booked for 18 months in advance. While he graciously offered to provide us with a time later in the following year, we knew it would not fit with our objective of having a mathematics-related author for the grand opening of the library exhibit. We moved on to David Schwartz and ascertained that the honorarium was more than we felt we should spend.

After checking our resources more thoroughly, we realized we had overlooked a perfect choice—Loreen Leedy. Even though we found out that she lived in Florida, we contacted the publicist, Diane Foote at Holiday House, who was very helpful and immediately conveyed our phone invitation to Leedy. Within a couple of days, we had a deal: Loreen Leedy would come to our area for three-and-a-half days. Foote drew up the letter of agreement, and we were set to begin our preparations for the visit.

Throughout all negotiations, it is helpful to keep an accurate phone log of all calls, including calls to directory information. (See Forms 9 and 10, "Phone Log" and "Directory Information Inquiry Log," in Section 8, page 99 and 100.) This log will help you determine the actual cost of your search as well as maintain a record of phone numbers and contacts so you can avoid duplicate calls and make follow-up calls. Note e-mail addresses on the "notes" line of the log pages.

The first author I ever attempted to arrange to come to our area was Marilyn Sachs. I first contacted the publishing house that had published her most recent book. I obtained the phone number from telephone information and called the publicist. The publicist did not know

## MARILYN SACHS
*What My Sister Remembered*
*Jojo & Winnie: Sister Stories*

Fifteen years after her visit to our community, Marilyn Sachs wrote that she has "been productive. Since my visit I have written 19 new books. I was also lucky enough to be a co-editor and contributor to *The Big Book for Peace* (Dutton, 1991), which raised a half million dollars for five selected peace organizations." Her knack for writing of family situations, particularly stories of sibling interaction, led to a popular series of books featuring Jojo and Winnie. The first book, *Jojo & Winnie: Sister Stories* (Dutton), was published in 1999, and a second title, *Jojo & Winnie Again: More Sister Stories* (Dutton), followed in 2000.

## PATRICIA POLACCO
*Thunder Cake*
*Welcome Comfort*
*Thank You, Mr. Falker*
*Pink and Say*
*The Butterfly*
*The Keeping Quilt*

"I have always been an artist—I could draw perspective drawings when I was four . . . later we learned that I am learning-disabled. I have dyslexia. This meant that reading was difficult and mathematics impossible! So art was the only thing that I felt I did well. When I got the help needed to learn I started to excel academically . . . but I remember as a child feeling that I was dumb . . . it was very painful. I imagine that is why I daydreamed so much of the time. In my imagination I was safe and smart and could do anything!"
—Patricia Polacco

Patricia Polacco writes many stories from her childhood in Michigan and later in California. She also writes family history stories, telling about her immigrant grandparents, their move from Russia to New York to Michigan, and finally her move with her mother and brother to California. Her stories give readers much information about the struggles of a family of immigrant Russian Jews and their assimilation into American society. Some of her family stories come from a grandfather's experiences during the Civil War (*Pink and Say* (Philomel, 1994), and *The Butterfly* (Philomel, 2000), which is based on the experiences of the author's great aunt, Marcel Solliliage, in France during World War II. After living in California for many years, Polacco and her two children moved back to Michigan where Polacco lives just down the road from the farm where she visited her grandparents as a child. Her son, Steven, and daughter, Tracy, live nearby. Steven maintains her Web site at <http://www.patriciapolacco.com>.

whom I was talking about and, frankly, did not seem interested in even talking to me about any author. Sachs was not a Newbery winner, but she certainly was popular enough to warrant the publicist's knowing her. Not to be rebuffed, I checked the book flaps of her books for biographical information. I learned that she lived in San Francisco, and I learned her husband's name. Even today many phone numbers are listed only in the man's name. I was able to obtain a San Francisco phone directory at the public library.

No entries were under "Marilyn Sachs," but I did locate three under her husband's name. I dialed the first number and told the person who answered why I was calling and that I was trying to locate the author Marilyn Sachs to inquire about an author visit. The response was "Oh, that's my Mom. She's at the library but will be home in a half an hour or so. If you'd like to leave your name and number, I'll ask her to call." That conversation took place over 20 years ago. Times have changed now. If I were searching for Marilyn Sachs today, I would go to my favorite online Web site at <http://www.555-1212.com> and key in a search for Sachs in San Francisco, California. With that search, I got 58 hits. I then added the "M" initial in the first name, and the search engine returned an entry listing both her and her husband's name. The process took less than five minutes.

I still find some publicists are unaware of authors or illustrators I am interested in locating. I find that if I cannot make the right connections at a publishing house, research in some of the standard reference sources or on the World Wide Web will yield a home address (and subsequently a phone number). If I contact an author or illustrator and that person prefers that I contact a publicist, she will give me the name and number of that person. Patricia Polacco at times has actually had a message on her answering service that begins, "If you are calling about a personal appearance, please call . . ."

Patricia and Fredrick McKissack seem to prefer to schedule through a publicist at one of their publishing houses. After the initial arrangements are made, they correspond directly. Their schedules are so full that one must often arrange for their visit over a year in advance. Tomie dePaola has a personal assistant who does all of his bookings—and he is booked two years or more in advance. Jack Prelutsky's wife, Carolynn, arranges his schedule, as does Eric A. Kimmel's wife, Doris. Each of them also works with publicists at his publishing house.

Some authors prefer not to make commitments more than six months in advance. The best advice I can give is to contact the publicist at the appropriate publishing house, ascertain the publicist's role, and go from there. Sometimes I have called a publicist to request a specific author only to find out that the author's honorarium has recently risen above our budget, but then I am able to ask the publicist to suggest authors who are currently making school visits. That is how I came to arrange for a visit by Nicholasa Mohr. At the time, she was just beginning to be recognized as an author for her accounts of life in El Barrio—Spanish Harlem. Her visit to our community was a major success.

Among those who regularly arrange for author/illustrator visits there is some discussion as to the appropriateness of telephoning an author/illustrator at home. Some state that they would not ever call an author/illustrator on the phone. At one time I would have concurred, but

### NICHOLASA MOHR
*Nilda*
*Felita*
*Going Home*

Nicholasa (Golpé) Mohr grew up in El Barrio of New York. Her parents (who emigrated from Puerto Rico) and her six brothers faced prejudice and struggled economically. But Mohr refused to lower her goals to meet others' low expectations. She became an artist whose work was exhibited in major galleries. Later she became a celebrated novelist, writing books based on her growing up in El Barrio of New York. *Nilda* (Harper, 1973; Arte Público Press, 1986) was her first book. In 1989, Mohr was awarded an honorary Doctor of Letters by the State University of New York. Her message when she speaks is to set goals high and to work toward them regardless of the perceptions of others. The girl from the Barrio, the girl who was counseled to learn some practical skills so she would not be a burden to society, is an accomplished artist and a celebrated writer because she knew she could succeed.

over the years I have heard from many authors/illustrators who are pleased that they have been called. They feel that their publishing house publicist is overworked and does not necessarily have time to devote to booking school visits or conference appearances for them; thus, many welcome the opportunity to respond to direct invitations. Those who do wish to have their visits scheduled by their publicists will say so.

Some authors, such as Roland Smith, make a large portion of their income through author visits. Smith, for example, actively promotes himself for visits and includes information on his Web site at <http://www.rolandsmith.com>. While he is on the road, his wife Marie handles some of his communications. It's not unusual to get an answer to an e-mail message from Marie with a later follow-up message from Roland. He knows the value of public relations, and as a result, he is booked throughout the year.

Fred Bowen is another author who does an exceptional job of promoting himself. Some authors actively solicit visits while other authors simply accept the offers that come their way and that appeal to them.

David McPhail, for example, dislikes the "book tour" and only seldom agrees to go on any tour to promote a book. For that reason, he rarely visits schools. During one book tour sponsored by his publisher, he did visit a school in the Midwest and drew illustrations of his popular bear character. He seemed to enjoy his young audience. It seems he just does not like the time the traveling takes away from his family and work.

One author of children's and young adult mystery and suspense novels was told by her New York publishing house editor that school visits are the most effective thing she could do to boost her popularity among young readers. However, nothing came of this particular author's request that the publicist schedule school visits for her. By being responsive to the telephone calls she receives at her home number and to inquiries made through her Web site, the author has been able to book many appearances on her own. Consequently she welcomes phone calls and e-mail inquiries about her availability for author visits. It is a source of additional income that does, indeed, boost her popularity.

In an article, "Results from the SCBWI Questionnaire On School Visits," published in *The Society of Children's Book Writers and Illustrators SCBWI Bulletin* (Dec. 1993/Jan. 1994, p. 4), Maryann Cocca-Leffler reported statistics that indicated, of those responding, almost 85 percent of the author/illustrators arranged their own school visits. Only 23 percent of responding authors/illustrators were ever booked for school visits by their publisher, and only 15 percent of the authors/illustrators have school visits set up by their publishers exclusively.

All things considered, it is, I believe, more advantageous to make arrangements through a publicist. However, if you have difficulty contacting a publicist, I would not hesitate to contact the author/illustrator directly—by phone, e-mail, or U.S. mail. Do not, however, make an inquiry of a publicist and then get impatient and make your own contact. Decide how you are going to contact the author and stick with it. If the publicist is not getting back to you, you might contact her and tell her that you have a deadline and you must know by a certain date. If you get no response, then you will have to make alternative inquiries.

Authors/illustrators who do not wish to be contacted will certainly say so, and those requests should be fully respected. In a response to a letter to Stephen Gammell asking about his availability for author visits, he wrote, "I thank you for your kind letter. However, I don't really care for publicity of any kind and am uncomfortable talking about myself." The writer respected Gammell's statement and made no further contact.

In another instance, a phone call to Eric Kimmel's residence resulted in a conversation with his wife, Doris Kimmel, who arranges his author visits. In five minutes, Doris Kimmel and the caller made tentative arrangements for him to speak at an author brunch in conjunction with a state reading association's conference to be held in ten months. Several days later, Kimmel made a firm commitment and written confirmation soon followed.

In another instance, Lisa Campbell Ernst gave a caller preliminary information regarding her willingness to participate in school visits, thanked her sincerely for being interested in her work, and referred the caller to a publicist at one of her publishing houses.

In none of these situations did the author convey displeasure at being contacted. In fact, quite the opposite was true. Authors/illustrators have the same range of personalities and likes and dislikes as anyone else, so it is conceivable that some will dislike any phone communication that they do not initiate. Others will prefer to be contacted by phone rather than in writing or by e-mail.

It is wise to begin at least a year in advance of any author/illustrator visit date. You might be lucky enough a get a firm commitment for an author/illustrator to visit your community in as little as one hour, but it more often takes several months. The length of time depends on the particular author/illustrator or publicist with whom you are working. In general, I have found that working with a publicist has the advantage of eliminating from your list of possibilities authors/illustrators who are not available. However, the trade-off is often in the time it takes for you to communicate with the publicist and the publicist with the author/illustrator, and back again to you.

### Eric A. Kimmel
*Anansi and the Talking Melon*
*Hershel and the Hanukkah Goblins*
*Easy Work!: An Old Tale*

"Few of my books are stories I heard as a child. What I acquired when I was young was a love of stories as well as an inner sense of what made a good one, or at least what made stories work for me. My grandmother told some good ones. So did my father. My two favorite books were a collection of Grimm's Fairy Tales and a gloriously illustrated edition of the Old Testament. I read both until they fell to pieces. I love a good story. I enjoy telling stories to an audience, but my ambition was always to be an author."
— Eric A. Kimmel

On each night of Hanukkah, Eric Kimmel's grandmother retold a Jewish folk tale from her childhood. Eric Kimmel sometimes tells of the origin of the Anansi tales that he tells. The first two tales were based on folk literature that he adapted and retold. However, the illustrator, Janet Stevens, and Kimmel actually collaborated on the story plot for *Anansi and the Talking Melon* (Holiday House, 1994). Eight years after that title was published, Holiday House plans to publish a fourth book in the series, *Anansi and the Talking Stick*, in 2002.

In a few instances, authors do not wish to make commitments too far in advance since they do not know exactly where they will want to be or what other commitments will be necessary. Most will commit at least six months in advance. There are also some authors/illustrators who are well known for making commitments but canceling a few weeks before the planned visit. There is absolutely no way of guarding against that. Even if the contract is in writing, situations beyond your or the author's control can occur.

For example, one year a state reading organization had contracted with a well-known author of intermediate and young adult books to be the keynote speaker at one of the biggest events of their conference. However, a couple of weeks earlier, the author was in Las Vegas and was mugged. Doctors ordered her not to travel for a month. The trip to the conference was out. Fortunately, the conference directors had some backup ideas and were able to obtain a replacement—a replacement who incidentally wowed the audience.

Frankly, keynote speakers for conferences are a little easier to replace that classroom guests. If one is in a school setting and an author cancels, because of all the preparatory reading of the author's books and related work, another author might not be an adequate replacement. It might be better to plan an alternative culmination to the unit, such as a video conference or e-mail chat combined with a celebration of another sort.

Perhaps the substitute event could be a whole day celebrating the author's work (in absentia) with book discussions, pseudo radio interviews, productions of plays, and dramatic readings of the author's works. You could spend the day creating responses to the author's or illustrator's work. At the end of the day, pack up the videotapes of the productions, the photographs of the posters, and the books—or the items themselves—and send them off to the author. While this may not be quite as effective, the children will respond if the adults handle it as an opportunity for them to share. The key, however, is to be prepared with a back-up plan.

Patricia Hermes and Carol Gorman were at our school for a daylong reader's workshop conference. They met with students throughout the day. That evening they were to speak at a gathering for parents and those youngsters who wished to return. Shortly after school was let out, it started snowing. The flakes were large and moderate drifts began to form. We knew that our audience would be minimal, and it was. But we decided to go ahead with the evening's presentation as the event could not really be postponed.

The audience was indeed small—fewer than 30 people. We dropped the "formal" presentation idea and decided to arrange our chairs in a more casual circle and make the presentation more conversational in tone. The custodian on duty stopped by and generously agreed to take us on a tour of the underground tunnels in our school—tunnels just like the ones featured in one of Gorman's books. We had a great time and parents felt at ease. They asked questions, and their children did, too. We all felt like friends.

A potentially disastrous meeting was transformed into one of the most enjoyable evenings we could have imagined. Our principal commented, "It's really too bad that more people did not come." He had enjoyed the evening immensely. However, if more people had shown up, the whole evening would have probably taken a different turn.

## *Getting It in Writing*

Once verbal arrangements have been made with the publicist or with the author/illustrator directly, you should follow up with a written letter or contract confirming arrangements. The following information is important to include:

- Date(s) of scheduled visit
- Agreed-upon honorarium and expenses to be reimbursed
- Who will make transportation arrangements—author, publisher, or sponsoring organization—and how reimbursement will be handled
- Expectations for visit: Will presentations be to students, parent organization, librarians? Will there be autographing sessions, a staff welcoming reception, evening dinner with planning committee?
- Topic expected for each of the presentations
- Site of the visit
- When exactly the author/illustrator can expect fees and expenses to be paid

When the agreement is outlined in writing, ask the author/illustrator about any dietary restrictions and what equipment, such as slide or overhead projector, he will need. Make a microphone available if the visitor is speaking to more than 50 people in one session or giving more than one presentation.

This is the time also to ask for the information you will need for publicity:

- Title of any presentation to be given in special evening, Saturday, or conference appearances
- Photographs
- Biographical information if it is not available from standard resource books (Be sure to consult these references before you ask. See "Books About Authors and Illustrators" in Section 9, page 113-114.)

Get *everything* in writing. A written agreement should make clear what is expected of both the author/illustrator and the host organization.

Since many schools have access to legal counsel, it makes good sense to request that a simple but binding contract be drawn up and signed to protect both parties to the agreement. At the very least, a letter of agreement should be written and signed by both parties.

Several authors/illustrators regularly travel with their spouses. Jan Brett's husband, Joseph Hearn, often accompanies her on author/illustrator visits. Willo Davis Roberts, Joan Lowery Nixon, and Scott Corbett are among others who often travel with their partners. However, each of these artists is careful to disclose the travel arrangements prior to the actual visit and include any expected considerations in negotiating for the visit. A few author/illustrator guests, however, have been known to show up expecting lodging and meal expenses for their families and have even billed the host organization for travel expenses for the whole entourage.

As in any other business, some authors do not live up to commitments. One popular author speaking at a statewide conference for educators spent the entire 55 minutes of her presentation berating the audience for having students write to her and for expecting to tape record her presentation.

During the planning for one conference, the committee decided to extend an invitation to three authors/illustrators. One requested an honorarium that was more than the combined honoraria for the other two and would fly only first class. She was pleasant enough during informal exchanges, but her formal presentation to over 300 educators was dominated by frequent references to her concerns about flying and getting to the airport on time for her flight home. The planning committee learned the hard way that a high honorarium does not ensure a quality presentation.

In the early 1970s, Donna Harsh at Fort Hays State University (Kansas) was already a veteran at planning author/illustrator conferences. When I asked her to recommend some artists who might make good speakers for a conference I was helping to organize, she said two things that I try to remember whenever I am booking an author/illustrator for a day in my community:

- Authors/illustrators are good at what they do, but this does not automatically make them good speakers; and
- A guest who is successful in one situation (for example, speaking at Fort Hays) will not necessarily be right in another situation or on another day.

There is never a guarantee as to a speaker's success. I'll use my own experience as an example. I enjoyed one university professor's half-day presentation on children's book illustrators and illustrations so much that I recommended inviting her to speak at another large conference on children's and young adult literature. I was looking forward to the presentation and, based on my previous experience, actively encouraged others to attend. We were all disappointed when her presentation seemed like something from outer space. She seemed to be speaking a foreign language. I left wondering what it was about my previous encounter with her that I had enjoyed so much. I would have thought it was my memory shorting out except two colleagues who had been at the first workshop commented to me that they had been looking forward to her presentation, but now they could not understand why. So even a recommendation may not guarantee success.

For several years, another conference for librarians and educators structured its author/illustrator events around an evening lecture prior to the daylong conference. One of the authors received an additional stipend to present at the evening session. Paid for by a special lecture fund that honored a retired professor, the evening prelude was free to educators, librarians, students, and the general public. One year, the featured guest gave the same presentation at both the Friday evening and the Saturday conference sessions. Her failure to prepare two presentations caused the conference planners to discontinue the evening event.

Perhaps these gaffes could have been prevented by clearer communication or a firm contract stating each party's obligations. I don't write about them to discourage you from planning a visit but to stress that you need to plan carefully, put all arrangements in writing, and expect each party to live up to the contract or agreement.

On the other side, authors/illustrators have conveyed equally appalling tales of honoraria not paid until 12 months after their appearance, travel expenses going without reimbursement for months despite three requests for payment, hosts who schedule six or more presentations when the agreement clearly specified no more than four, requested equipment not available (or not working), and adult authorities who failed to reprimand disruptive or unprepared students.

One author/illustrator arrived in a community to find that the motel accommodations promised were actually a bedroom in a private home on the outskirts of the city, where he was expected to share a bathroom with three young children and two adults. On the way to the morning conference, his escort had to drive 15 miles to the childcare center to drop off a toddler before they could proceed to their destination.

In an effort to avoid problems with unprepared students and other disasters, some authors have begun to use a newsletter to acquaint those who book them with some of the ins and outs of arranging for a successful author/illustrator visit. Form 11, "Making the Most of an Author/Illustrator Visit: A Newsletter," in Section 8, pages 101-102 touches on some of these considerations. The planning committee can share this information with the entire staff of a school or other sponsoring organization.

In the course of arranging for more than a hundred author/illustrator visits, I have never personally encountered a disaster in terms of the guest's fulfilling expectations or obligations. In fact, the majority of visits have been much more than I had hoped for. I think being well-informed and prepared are key elements for a successful visit. Another important key is clear communication. No detail is too small to warrant attention.

## ▶ WHERE SHOULD YOU HOLD THE EVENT?

During school visits, it is usually best if the children come to the guest rather than move the guest from room to room. This allows for a more controlled atmosphere and in most cases, provides a more comfortable environment for the presentation.

In some situations, the committee may have to decide how many and which students will be involved in an author/illustrator visit, based on the space available. It is best, I think, to limit the number of students directly involved rather than attempt to crowd too large an audience into an inadequate space or expect the speaker to give multiple presentations to accommodate all of the students. If the library media center can accommodate large groups of children, it is a possibility. We have been able to use our library media center for presentations when only a portion of our student body is involved. When an author/illustrator has been invited to speak to just the primary classes (K-2), we divided the audience into three groups of 90 students each and accommodated them in the media center. We used the same venue when a novelist spoke to grades three through five. But we could not have held these events in the media center if either speaker had insisted on making only one presentation.

Sometimes a school has a multi-use room that can be dedicated to the author/illustrator presentations. When Craig McFarland Brown visited our school, we were able to use an auxiliary classroom normally used for individual student tutoring, small group instruction with gifted and talented students, volunteer readers to primary students, and a host of other incidental educational uses. Since stories illustrated by Brown include *My Barn* (Greenwillow, 1991) and Patricia Demuth's *Ornery Morning* (Dutton 1991), both set on a farm, intermediate classes converted the room into the interior of a barn, complete with a bale of hay and a saddle. Another class created the facade of a barn around the classroom door, flanking the doorway with a fence and animals. On another wall directly outside the room, another class drew the green pick-up truck used to drive to the city in Brown's *City Sounds* (Greenwillow, 1992). Not only did the activities involve research (discovering what a hen's nest looks like), mathematics (drawing each animal to the same scale), and creative thinking, but the final result contributed to the welcoming atmosphere for Brown's visit.

Some schools have used the cafeteria for large group meetings, but usually this is not the best location because the flooring is often noisier and the room is less aesthetically pleasing. However, a cafeteria can be decorated. Asking children to sit on the floor might not be a good idea, but asking children to carry their own chairs to the presentation has worked for several organizers. The crucial thing here is to get the first row placed where you want it and arrange the rest of the chairs in reference to that first row. We found out the hard way that folding chairs are too big for young children. During the presentation, they became intrigued with the way they could move the seats up and down with their legs, so the presentation was punctuated with the sound of seats being flipped up and down. On the other hand, molded school desk chairs work fine; they fit younger children's bodies much better. Mostly we just ask children to sit on the floor—often on carpet squares if the floor is tile.

Using the cafeteria requires some scheduling considerations. Custodians need ample time to set up for lunch and clean up afterward. Consult with affected school personnel to agree how the sessions can be handled with the least inconvenience for all concerned. Under no circumstances should anyone be putting up or taking down tables or should children be eating during a presentation in the cafeteria.

Sometimes the solutions to a space problem can come from an unexpected source. During the planning sessions for one author/illustrator visit, we realized we did not have a suitable location. The library media center was too small; our multi-use classroom was now a regular classroom; and our cafeteria has four large square pillars that preclude its use for a large group presentation. We have a large gymnasium, but the weather was too cold to hold physical education classes outdoors the day of the author's/illustrator's visit. We were stymied.

---

### JANET STEVENS
***Goldilocks and the Three Bears***
***How the Manx Cat Lost Its Tail***
***The Three Billy Goats Gruff***

"I always loved to draw animals, especially rhinoceros because they are so wrinkled. After a trip to Africa where I looked at all the funny animals, I went back to Colorado and drew camels wearing my shoes and a rhino wearing my clothes and lying on my rug. All of these are just pictures. They are waiting for words because words are a stage where my animals can dance."

—Janet Stevens (1990)

During presentations, Stevens often shows slides of her illustrations and tells about her family and their belongings that she has used as part of her illustrations. The animals in her illustrations wear articles of clothing that belong to her family and sit in the Stevenses' chairs. Her husband's tie and her little girl's bunny slippers show up in *The Tortoise and the Hare* (Holiday, 1981), and the three bears from *Goldilocks and the Three Bears* (Holiday, 1986) sit in the Stevenses' living room. Family members sometimes end up in her books.

But when we talked to other staff members about the problem, the physical education teacher offered to plan activities that could be handled in the classrooms for that day so the gymnasium could be used for the author/illustrator presentations. His generosity and cooperation showed his commitment to the total educational program. He also took over many supervisor duties in the lunchroom and on the playground that day to free other teachers to help their students make the most of the day. He displayed the type of cooperation that ideally is part of every author visit—in fact, every school-wide activity—in every school.

In some schools, the place to hold the sessions will be obvious. In others, the decision will take some thought. Don't overlook involving all the staff because someone may have a solution that should have been obvious but wasn't. When choosing the location for the presentations, be sure to consider

- Space per student. If you need to, have a trial run to determine if the space is adequate.
- Space for the speaker and needed equipment. Make sure the speaker has some space to move around.
- Visibility. Can the room be darkened sufficiently for slides? Are there visual barriers that will prevent some of the students from seeing the speaker?
- Availability of a sound system (almost a necessity if the audience is larger than 50).
- Acoustics. A carpeted floor reduces audience noise during the presentation.
- Seating. If children are going to sit on the floor, is it a floor they can sit on comfortably?

For author/illustrator presentations outside the school, you'll need to look at accommodations and consider the needs of the audience. For example, for a conversational meeting sponsored by a public library, a large meeting room furnished with ten round tables, each seating six guests, padded (and attractive) folding chairs, and a serving counter for light refreshments is ideal. A more formal evening function for a large group would require a different location—perhaps a gymnasium. High school or local college auditoriums are often available, for nonprofit events, for a nominal fee or just the cost of the custodians who must be on duty. If it's a school event, a facility in another school in the same system is usually free. Local colleges will sometimes contribute the use of a facility in return for credit as a cosponsor of the event.

Don't overlook large businesses that might have appropriate meeting rooms. Just recently I became aware of a wonderful facility in a local hospital that formerly had a nursing college. The dormitory-classroom building has been converted to offices, but the auditorium, seating 200, is still intact and available for community activities. It had been there all these years without my knowledge.

Most communities have a motel or hotel with a banquet room that can be used for day-long conferences. Some hotels will supply these facilities free or at a nominal cost in exchange for serving the meal. The meal fee will be higher than a nonprofit organization would charge, but if it includes the meeting room, it's worth considering. The conference or convention director at the hotel will work with the conference planners to set up the room as they want it. Since the hotel may charge extra for any audiovisual equipment it is asked to supply, the sponsors may wish to bring their own.

## Function of the Facility

For school events there must be spaces for the general sessions, for book sales, if planned, and for the guest author to autograph the books and to take a breather. Usually the biggest concern is accommodating the general sessions. The library media center is often a good site for autographing and book sales because it has book carts for holding books to be autographed and books already autographed and tables for the autographing and informal interaction with students.

For events outside the school, in addition to space for the general sessions, you may also need rooms for small group meetings (especially for a young author's day), for displaying and selling books, for autographing and picking up autographed books, and for lunch. Evaluate the traffic pattern between the general session and the lunch location, looking for potential bottlenecks. Develop a floor plan. A U-shaped design moves those wishing to purchase books around the room smoothly. Make adaptations and try different ideas, but on the day of the event (or the day before if possible) make sure the plan and the necessary tables are available and arrange to have helpers place the furniture according to the plan. (See Form 12 in Section 8, page 103.)

## Microphones and Sound Systems

When you expect a large group, the sound system is extremely important. Most auditoriums will be equipped with a sound system, but often gymnasiums are not. For rooms that do not have a built-in sound system, arrange for a portable sound system. Be aware that many speakers now prefer to use a wireless microphone rather than be tied to a stationary microphone. Audiovisual firms rent wireless microphones for a nominal fee that includes the mike itself, the transmitter that attaches to a belt or pocket, and the receiver that attaches to the existing sound system and amplifier.

Set up and test the equipment in ample time to make alternate arrangements if anything is not working properly. If possible, have a backup microphone available, even if it is a less desirable stationary or hand-held one.

## Technology

Find out early in the planning if the visiting author/illustrator requires any technological equipment. Arrange for this equipment well in

### GARY PAULSEN
*Hatchet*
*The River*
*The Crossing*

Gary Paulsen seldom uses visuals when he presents. His personality is larger than life, but when he speaks to very large audiences, he needs a microphone. Regarding the responses he gets from his presentations, he says, "Kids ask a lot of pretty basic questions. 'How long does it take to write a book?' and 'I'm interested in writing. How can I get into it?' The question I am asked most frequently is 'What is the most important thing to do if you want to become a writer?' The answer is, of course, to read. But sometimes I hit a nerve or they hit a nerve. During one speech I mentioned that my son (Jim) doesn't like to read my work. A kid wrote and asked, 'Weren't you hurt that your son didn't want to read your work?' I could see that nobody was listening to this kid. After *Winterkill* (Thomas Nelson, 1976) came out, I got a lot of letters about drunk parents."

— Gary Paulsen

advance of the day to make sure it's available. The most requested pieces of equipment are overhead and slide projectors.

Make sure you have a spare bulb for each piece of equipment that may need one; better yet, have an additional piece of equipment available. If a bulb blows out on a projector, for example, it is a simple matter to unplug the projector and replace it with the second one. Once the blown-out bulb cools down, it can be replaced and the first projector held as backup to the second one.

Of course, an extra bulb for any piece of equipment is of little use if no one knows how to put it in the machine. Some overhead projectors are now being manufactured with a dual bulb system. If the first bulb blows out, you slide the replacement bulb door over and continue projecting.

Let the following story serve as a caveat to check the equipment yourself or have someone you trust implicitly check it. A planning committee arranged to use a large high school's facilities for a Saturday children's literature conference to be attended by more than 300 teachers and library media specialists. The high school library media specialist was to place a slide projector in the auditorium, along with an extra projection bulb. Early on Saturday morning, a student assistant set up the equipment. During the speaker's presentation, the slide projector's bulb blew out. Unfortunately, the extra bulb was for another model slide projector. The speaker did her best (quite successfully) to proceed with alternative examples while members of the planning committee attempted to track down someone with a key to the library media center's cabinet containing the replacement bulbs. It took them half an hour to locate an assistant principal who just happened to be in the building. Luckily, he had access to a key to the cabinet.

No detail is too incidental to check. If possible, ask those who have a vested interest in the success of the event to check out specific details. If you are using a facility that is not your own, you may be better off bringing your own equipment. You'll be assured of its condition and familiar with how it works. And you'd be sure to have replacement bulbs of the correct type.

If the group is large and the slide projector is on a cart in the center of the audience, the speaker will not have direct access to the control for advancing the slides or backing them up when she needs to. She'll either have to signal someone to move the slides or speak from the center of the room where she also can control the slides. A cordless remote control or a remote control extension cord would allow her to remain at the podium and still advance the slides. If the speaker is making multiple presentations in your area, you could carry a standard remote cord from site to site. If you are using a cordless remote, be sure it is compatible with all of the slide projection equipment at the various sites.

Since the speaker will not have used the equipment before, be sure someone is present who *does* know the equipment. One author tells of the time she started slides with a remote control, but once she began speaking it became apparent that the slide projector had a mind of its own. The slides began to move, seemingly on their own. Nothing the author could do from the stage changed the pattern. Staff members tried in vain to correct the problem. Fortunately the slides were only the introduction of her presentation. Between the first and second presentations, an adept student who often helped in the library media center took a look at the projector and discovered that the automatic advance was on, which made the projector advance every ten seconds.

If the room is going to be darkened for any type of image projection, provide a small light at the podium area to enable the speaker to read notes. If the podium does not have a built-in light, provide a small flashlight. The optimum would be a small battery-operated light that would stand on the podium, leaving the speaker's hands free. Alternatively, notch a small box to hold a regular flashlight at the correct angle for reading. And be sure to check out the way it works and how it will function when the room is darkened.

The last, but certainly not the least, item to be concerned with is the projection screen. Use the largest screen available. Check its condition and, if necessary, clean it. On the day of the presentation, someone should be available to pull down or set up the screen and arrange the equipment the way the speaker wants it. Many auditoriums now have wall screens that can be pulled down. If your presentation room is equipped with such a screen, be sure you have access to the controls. In schools, those controls are often in a locked or restricted room.

## *Lunch and Amenities*

If lunch is included, plan it well in advance. For conferences held on a school or college campus, the food service will often cater a meal for a minimal price. If this is not possible, consider contracting with an outside caterer. We have had great success offering boxed lunches. You can include the lunch in the price of the conference registration or sell lunch tickets to those who want them. All lunches should be reserved in advance. If the food service staff is going to serve the meal, it should be located convenient to the kitchen as well as to the general sessions.

A reserved table or places should be marked for the speaker or speakers and their hosts, as well as any workers who will be busy up to the minute lunch is served. They should be served first, so they are finished before anyone else. The speakers can then return to autographing books, preparing for their presentation, or socializing with the conference participants. The workers, of course, will return to their stations.

You can make the lunch more festive by giving it a theme based on the author's/illustrator's books, with centerpieces, place mats, and programs that reflect the theme. While a theme is probably not the most important ingredient in making the event a success, it provides an additional avenue for children's responses to literature.

Several authors/illustrators report that they appreciate a potluck luncheon provided by the school staff because it lets them sample local dishes, adds a touch of informality, and involves the entire staff in welcoming the speaker. A potluck luncheon should, of course, be held away from the children. This should be a time when the speaker can relax and enjoy meeting some of the adults in the building.

Another alternative is to offer the school lunch to the guest. This is especially appropriate if the luncheon has been planned with the guest in mind. Some schools have planned a menu based on the author's/illustrator's favorite foods. For example, one of Craig Brown's favorite foods is salad, and he prefers vegetables, so on the day of his visit, the school lunch featured chef's salads filled with vegetables. Other times, the luncheon could be based on foods that are part of the author's books. A visit by Keiko Kasza, author of *The Wolf's Chicken Stew* (Putnam, 1987), might inspire a meal that readers envision the chicken serving the wolf at the end of the book—and that would NOT be chicken stew. But it might include the chocolate chip cookies the wolf takes to the hen's little chickens. When Beatrice Schenk de Regniers visited, her book, *How Joe the Bear and Sam the Mouse Got Together* (Lothrop, Lee & Shepard Books, 1990), provided the idea for the cafeteria staff to plan a meal complete with ice cream. Don't go overboard with the book food idea, though. One author stopped mentioning that his favorite color was purple as he had been served everything from purple cabbage to purple macaroni on school visits.

Other options include lunch in a nearby restaurant or a catered lunch. Some authors/illustrators enjoy eating lunch with the students, while others welcome conversation with the adult staff. Courtesy dictates asking the author/illustrator her preference.

Restrooms for use when an author/illustrator visits a school should not be a problem unless it involves parents and members of the community. Other types of author/illustrator events may present a problem because many locations don't have adequate restroom facilities to handle 200 to 300 persons during relatively short break times. Try to choose a location that has as many restroom facilities as possible. This is discussed further in Section 5.

# SECTION 4

# The Author/Illustrator Focus

## ▶ IMPORTANCE OF PREPARING THE AUDIENCE

Once the arrangements are made and confirmed in writing, it is time to implement the rest of the plan. The most successful author/illustrator school visits have usually followed an author/illustrator focus of two to three months, but shorter focus times have succeeded, too. One October a school staff learned that an author would be in the area with a free day he could spend at their school. It was an opportunity they could not pass up. They understood the importance of preparation and devoted much of their classroom time to integrating the author's books into curriculum activities. They read his books, wrote innovations on the text, studied his style of illustrating, tried their own hand at illustrating, learned about the author's life and what part that background played in his books. They immersed themselves in his books for several days. When the author came, the children were eager and attentive. They knew what questions they wanted to ask, and the questions were appropriate.

The audience must be prepared and the visit viewed as a culmination of a celebration of the author's/illustrator's books. The celebration (or focus unit) of the author's/illustrator's work incorporates many reading and writing activities and integrates those activities into other curriculum areas. Each of the activities suggested corresponds to an existing curriculum goal or objective.

Author visits sponsored by other organizations, such as public libraries, art museums, and reading associations, will require a different type of preparation. In these settings, much

### JACQUELINE BRIGGS MARTIN
*Snowflake Bentley*
*The Lamp, the Ice, and the Boat Called Fish: Based on a True Story*
*Button, Bucket, Sky*

Since her book *Snowflake Bentley* earned the Caldecott Award for Mary Azarian's bold and dramatic woodcut illustrations, Martin has enjoyed many invitations to visit schools across the United States. The level of preparation is usually very evident. She says, "When I visit a school and the children's questions consist mostly of, 'How much money do you make?' 'What books have you written?' or 'How old are you?' it is usually a first indication of the level of preparation and involvement the young audience has had with my books."

—Jacqueline Briggs Martin

of the preliminary preparation will be in developing ways to acquaint potential participants with the author's/illustrator's books. Promotion will be the major thrust.

Daniel Pinkwater describes a humorous worst-case scenario for an author visit in *Author's Day* (Macmillan, 1993). When the author arrives, it is clear that everyone has confused the title of a book he has written with one that he has not, and all of the day's activities and references are to the wrong book. Pinkwater says that his work is pure fiction. Such a case of mistaken identity has never happened to him. But some authors have experienced situations too similar to those he describes.

One author arrived at a school and was directed to the room where she would be speaking. She was not given a schedule; the children who arrived did not seem to be aware of why she had come, and they did not know any of the books she had written. At the break for lunch, she had to find her own way to the staff lounge. No one offered to arrange lunch for her. For that matter, no one even conversed with her.

Another author visited a school where the staff was somewhat more gracious, but it appeared that the children had not read even one of his books. They had questions for him, such as, "What books have you written?" "Are you famous?" "How come I have never heard of any of your books?" and "Why do you go to schools?" He left wondering why he did visit that school.

Planning and preparation will prevent the author's/illustrator's day from becoming one of those on the dark side of the ledger when the publicists or authors/illustrators discuss your community.

## ▶ PLANNING THE FOCUS

Planning and preparation cannot be overemphasized. Careful planning can make the visit run as smoothly and be as rewarding as possible for you, the audience, and your guest. Preparing the audience and preliminary planning for any public event are crucial.

As you plan the focus, keep in mind the goals and objectives for the visit itself. In school visits, pay particular attention to curriculum objectives that you can meet through activities involving the author's/illustrator's books. Focusing on an author/illustrator and using literature in the classroom or library are not as simple as gathering together activity suggestions for the author's/illustrator's books. There is no reason that the focus should not be tied to the goals and objectives of the school curriculum, library, or museum program.

If you keep the goals and objectives in mind, you can select activities to reach them. In schools, you can develop activities using the visiting author's books and incorporating activities from standard sources: basal reader manuals, a language arts text, or a prescribed curriculum manual for your district. Other types of sponsors might develop programs focusing on an element of the author's/illustrator's work; for example, an art museum might emphasize the illustrator's technique while a local council of the International Reading Association may use the author's work to motivate reading.

## ▷ COLLABORATING TO MAKE CONNECTIONS

You can find suggestions for activities and goal or objective tie-ins in resource books developed specifically for author/illustrator visits. Such books are not the only source of information, but they provide a starting point to use in conjunction with brainstorming sessions. An author/illustrator visit is an opportunity to bring educators together to brainstorm ideas and figure out how to integrate them into established curriculum.

When Beatrice Schenk de Regniers visited our community, we developed many suggestions for focusing on her books and published them in a "resource book" that all teachers in all the schools she was to visit could use. In the resource book for de Regniers' *Catch a Little Fox: Variations on a Folk Rhyme* (Clarion, 1970), one teacher noticed a suggestion for comparing this book to John Langstaff's *Oh, A-Hunting We Will Go* (Atheneum, 1974). The suggestion, which included critical reading activities and innovative writing projects, called to her mind traditional song and dance instructions in *Frank Schaffer's Schooldays* (Nov./Dec./Jan.1986-87, p. 17).

The resource book had served two of its purposes: to suggest some appropriate activities and to call up prior knowledge that might suggest additional activities.

No one resource book can be all things to all audiences. Its purpose is mainly to give basic suggestions, to help teachers and librarians recall prior knowledge, to give background information about the author/illustrator, and to suggest tie-ins between the author's/illustrator's work and other materials. The resource book attempts to provide the type of information that many would otherwise have to locate in lists of collaborative readings for thematic tie-ins (complete with bibliographic information), and references to other available sources of information.

That is also the goal of commercial resources that suggest ways to use books of selected authors/illustrators. (See "Books About Authors and Illustrators" in Section 9, page 113-114.) Sometimes they include ideas for extension activities or inspire you to develop your own. Professional periodicals, such as *Teaching Pre K-8, Instructor, Frank Schaffer's Schooldays, Library Talk, The Book Report*, and *Booklinks,* often feature interviews with authors and illustrators, and many of these interviews include suggestions for responding to the author's/illustrator's books.

Dozens of World Wide Web sites provide basic information about authors, and many authors maintain their own Web sites. Sites such as Jim Aylesworth's site at <http://www.ayles.com> provide not only information about his books but also suggestions for correlating his books with writing, other curricular areas, and further reading. (See the extensive list of author Web sites in Section 9, page 118-119.)

Many publishers include information about authors and books on their sites. Some publishers include links and information that may help teachers to connect books with other classroom activities. For example, HarperCollins (http://www.harpercollins.com) offers teaching guides for many of its books. The guides can be downloaded as a PDF (Portable Document Format) file. You will need to install Adobe Acrobat Reader on your computer to allow you to read PDF files. If the reader is not built into your Web browser, it can be downloaded for free from the Adobe site at <http://www.adobe.com>.

Other publishers offer suggestions online. For example, Harcourt (<http://www.harcourt.com>) has a search feature for searching for authors by name or book title. For example, Eve Bunting's *Flower Garden* is available as a big book, and a page (<http://www.harcourt.com/parents/recommended_reads/flower_garden.html>) on the Harcourt site is linked from the title and provides several suggestions for using the book with students.

## ▶ PREPARING A RESOURCE BOOKLET

The planning committee can generate a resource booklet, or a group of interested staff members might work on a separate project to develop a resource booklet for the visit. Ideally the resource book acquaints those who are planning activities with the author/illustrator's books and gives background about the author's/illustrator's life. It also serves as a "collection place" to list resources that will be valuable for others who are working to prepare for the author/illustrator visit.

When activities were being planned for a visit by David Wisniewski, who creates his art by cutting paper, one teacher spotted a pertinent article by Jane Rhoades in *Teaching Pre K-8* (May 1993, p. 70). The article, "Teaching Art: 'Drawing' with Scissors and Paper," discusses Henri Matisse's ability to "draw" with a large pair of scissors even when he was bedridden. The result was his now-famous cutout series. The article explained how teachers could introduce the idea of paper cuts by making shadow puppets and silhouettes and later progressing to paper cuts. This article helped everyone prepare for Wisniewski's visit. Now those preparing for a visit by Wisniewski can utilize his own book about shadow theater, *Worlds of Shadows: Teaching with Shadow Puppetry* (Libraries Unlimited, 1996). Educators and young readers will enjoy using some of his shadow puppetry techniques both before and after his visit.

## *Building on the Ideas of Others*

A resource booklet for a specific author/illustrator's school visit should include four basic steps: planning an introductory activity; creating a thematic web for each of the books written/illustrated by the author/illustrator; using the web to plan activities; and planning a culminating activity for use after the author's/illustrator's visit.

Other sponsors may wish to develop a variation of the resource book. At times the resource book's suggestions could also be adapted for use in other situations. For example, the Iowa Reading Association regularly sponsors an author/illustrator presentation as the Saturday morning brunch feature attraction during its annual spring conference. Schools in the surrounding area often opt to invite the same author to their school on days preceding the reading association's event. The reading association promotes the author's/illustrator's appearance to its 4,500 members in the state by announcing the guest artist as a headline speaker in its newspaper (published three or four times a year). In conjunction with that announcement, a separate column often highlights background information on the author/illustrator and suggests ways to incorporate the author's/illustrator's books into classroom activities. (See the following sample activities.) These are intended to be "starter" suggestions; you will need to modify or expand them to meet goals and objectives for your specific group.

### SAMPLE ACTIVITIES

Eric A. Kimmel, *Baba Yaga: A Russian Folktale*. Illustrated by Megan Lloyd. Holiday, 1991.

Baba Yaga is a traditional Russian folktale character. When Marina goes to Baba Yaga to ask Baba to remove a horn from her forehead, Baba attempts to trick her into becoming her dinner. Marina manages to escape through the help of those she had been kind to while she was on her way to Baba's hut.

- Locate other tales that feature Baba Yaga and develop a profile of this folktale character. See especially *Babushka Baba Yaga* by Patricia Polacco (Philomel, 1993).
- Discuss the major theme of the tale and then compare and contrast the tale to *The Talking Eggs* by Robert San Souci, illustrated by Jerry Pinkney (Dial, 1989).

— From Iowa Reading (Fall, 1993); Reprinted with permission.

At various times the Cedar Rapids Art Museum has hosted individual exhibits of the work of such renowned illustrators as Tomie dePaola, Jan Brett, Shonto Begay, and Peter Sis. A combined exhibit focused on the work of Jerry Pinkney, Brian Pinkney and writers Gloria Pinkney and Andrea Davis Pinkney. In preparation for the opening of each of these exhibits, the art museum staff prepared a resource booklet for visitors that contained background information on the artist and his work and suggestions for becoming acquainted with his books and for a focus on the artwork created for the books. The museum held a workshop for teachers and other interested adults prior to the exhibit's opening day and distributed the resource booklet to all participants.

Tomie dePaola was present at the workshop to autograph books, answer questions, and speak about work in progress and future projects. Eric Carle was unable to visit but sent his personal assistant to the workshop to answer participants' questions. Jan Brett came dressed in an outfit complete with red cowboy boots like those the main character wears in *Armadillo Rodeo* (Putnam, 1995). She told the workshop participants how she got the idea and the research she did for both the text and the illustrations.

We were able to use much of the information she shared to incorporate her books into our classrooms. For example, during her presentation, Brett shared some information about armadillos: Litters of armadillos always come in fours, and all four are the same sex; armadillos are very near-sighted. Such armadillo facts figure into the picture book, and we were able to use them to incorporate her book into a third grade study of animals. In an afternoon reception that highlighted Peter Sis's visit, he commented on each of the illustrations in the exhibit.

These author/illustrator events were planned for an adult audience, but they directly affected children who would be prepared for a visit to the exhibit. Adults who attended these presentations and receptions learned important background information they could use to prepare their students. Sis, who uses his Czech background in *Tibet Through the Red Box* (Farrar Straus Giroux, 1998), told us about the history of the Czech Republic and how his father, a Czech filmmaker, came to be in Tibet. Sis's own life story gave us insight into the political climate in the Czech Republic. We were able to use Sis's books to prepare for a visit to the National Czech and Slovak Museum, which was part of the activities suggested in social studies curriculum.

Each resource booklet prepared by the museum contained biographical articles from the publisher or from other resources (reprinted with permission) and included citations to other resources about the author/illustrator and his books. The booklets, each approximately 90 pages, also contained information about the exhibit, including what original art pieces were included and in which books those pieces appear.

Public libraries that sponsor author/illustrator visits will have a slightly different take on the need to promote books as preparation for an author/illustrator event. Many public libraries advertise the day and time of the author's presentation—and that's it. The visit *is* the event. Other libraries extend the visit with promotional sessions. In conjunction with Loreen Leedy's visit to the Cedar Rapids (Iowa) Public Library, the library joined with the local area education agency to sponsor two teacher workshops and an open house for the community where children and adults could hear brief comments by the author, meet her, get autographed books, and tour a related exhibit.

One library held a two-hour morning seminar with resource speakers presenting the author's/illustrator's books, reading from them, suggesting how the books could inspire readers to investigate other topics, and asking the participants to brainstorm other connections that could be made with the author's/illustrator's books. The group developed thematic webs and distributed copies. Following a lunch hour, the guest author gave a presentation and responded to questions from the audience. The evaluations of the presentation event clearly showed that the morning seminar enhanced it. Since members of the audience had discussed the author/illustrator and her books, her presentation and the questions it generated could enhance knowledge already established.

In school situations, funding for the development of the booklets might be available through grants for curriculum design. You might include the printing cost in the miscellaneous allocation in the budget or sell individual copies for a fee to offset the cost. If you offer the booklet as part of a seminar or workshop on the author's/illustrator's books, include the cost for the booklet in the seminar fee.

Organizations with in-house production facilities will be able to duplicate the booklets for much less than a commercial printer would charge. Sometimes a business concern will consider donating printing at cost as part of its contribution to the author visit.

In schools, these resource booklets will become a primary source for activities that will help teachers and students reach curriculum goals while focusing on the prospective visitor's work. In other settings, the booklet could serve as a promotion vehicle or a resource for other adults who work with children.

## Using Book Webs

Once sessions get under way for planning curriculum connections and generating ideas for integrating the author/illustrator's books into curriculum goals, gather as many of the author's/illustrator's books as are available to your committee and staff. To develop resource suggestions, project planners must have access to as many of the author's/illustrator's books as possible. Search local libraries for existing titles and make arrangements at once to purchase other titles.

Make a master list of the titles available, including complete bibliographic information, and make a note as to the where each of the books can be obtained (school library, public library). Depending on the number of books, this process may take several sessions.

At the time David Wisniewski was to be the featured author/illustrator at our schools, he had published four titles. Each member of the committee could easily read all four and be involved in the brainstorming for each title. When one school hosted Gloria Skurzynski, the committee found that she had published novels, picture books, and several nonfiction titles. Each member of the committee selected titles to read thoroughly and later shared the book's content through booktalks with others on the planning committee.

We generated activities for each of the books after creating a book web for each of the

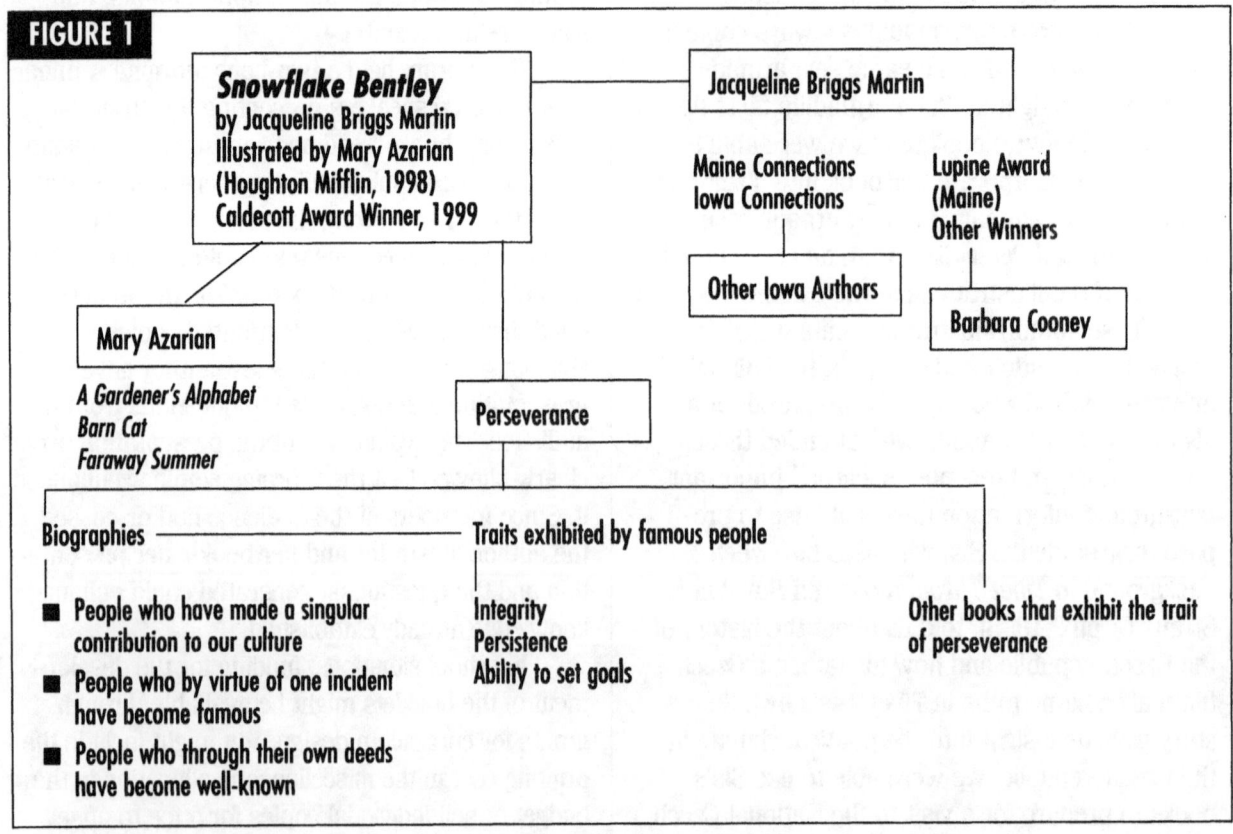

FIGURE 1

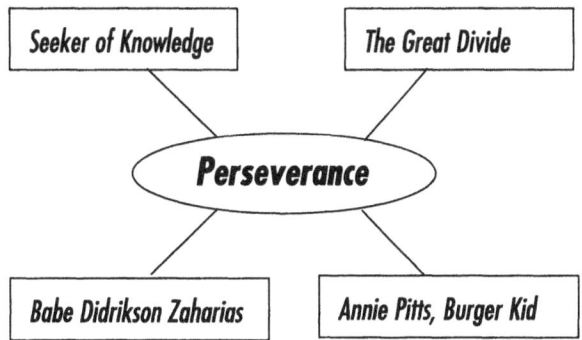

FIGURE 2  A THEMATIC WEB: PERSEVERANCE

- Dodds, Dayle Ann. *The Great Divide*. Illustrated by Tracy Mitchell. Candlewick Press, 1999.
- deGroat, Diane. *Annie Pitts, Burger Kid.* SeaStar, 2000.
- Rumford, James. *Seeker of Knowledge: The Man Who Deciphered Egyptian Hieroglyphs.* Houghton Mifflin, 2000.
- Freedman, Russell. *Babe Didrikson Zaharias.* Illustrated with photographs. Clarion Books, 1999.

titles. Those who had read the specific title took the lead in brainstorming to create the web of topics and themes for integrating that book into the curriculum. Once we generated the webbed topics, others in the group could supply information corresponding with each topic.

A book web can take many forms, from a wheel to a linear chain. Figure 1 is an example of a linear web created for a book written by Jacqueline Briggs Martin.

Make specific suggestions for each level of the web. The introductory segment for this book often includes a reading of the book and a discussion of the story, including the events that reveal Snowflake Bentley's character. There is clear evidence of his perseverance. He made many sacrifices to reach his goal, enduring many cold winter days to photograph snowflakes and other objects in nature. Use the web to suggest other activities or stories that form other connections to the perseverance component. Use examples of local community leaders or people the students know. Add other books with the theme of perseverance or persistence. (See Figure 2.)

You could include many other books in the activity suggestions for the other levels of the web for *Snowflake Bentley.* Discussions, murals, story maps, and readers' theater are some of the possible responses for any of the other books. Specific responses depend on the needs of the children and the teacher's objectives. One group writing project might involve researching the life of Bentley and filling in some of the facts and details that Martin chose not to include in her biography.

- How would his life have been different if his parents had not purchased his camera for him?
- Discuss other traits he exhibited and how those traits were shown in the book.
- How do other people display those traits?
- Read other books that focus on that trait.

Develop book webs and response suggestions for each of the author's/illustrator's books. Put the suggestions for using and responding to the various books in a format you can share with others involved in the visit. As teachers use the suggestions, they can modify or expand on them to make them as beneficial as possible to the young readers who will participate in the visit.

For books that are listed as collaborative readings or suggested as part of a connection, be sure to cite the author, title, illustrator, publisher, and copyright date.

## ▶ BRING ON THE BOOKS

If an author's/illustrator's visit is to be schoolwide, place copies of all available titles on reserve in the library. If the books are picture books, encourage children to come to the library to read the titles any time they can. Let them check out novels for a three- to five-day period. Both of these policies would allow as many children as possible to read the books. Obviously, you'll have to adapt that suggestion if some of the author's or illustrator's books are out-of-print or can't be purchased. Interlibrary loan is an option for these titles.

If possible, make a second copy of each book available for staff checkout for the minimum time they would need to introduce their students to the book. If they are using a book as a read-aloud, it could be shared any time of the day it wasn't being read aloud. Novels could be read aloud over a period of days. Several classrooms in a wing of a school could share a read-aloud title if each classroom had a different read-aloud time. Or schedule each of the books, on a rotating basis, into classrooms for a week at a time. Regardless of how you circulate books among the classrooms, make another copy of each book available so teachers can refer to it as they draw various connections between the focus author's books and those of other writers.

But it is not only the author's/illustrator's books that need to be available. Books for collaborative reading activities must be on hand as well. The key is to use the author's/illustrator's books to motivate students to read not only those books but also as many others as can possibly be connected to them.

Whatever procedure you use for getting the books into the right hands at the right time, make sure there are enough books so that all children can have the books read aloud, discuss them, and if possible, read the books for themselves. You might be able to purchase some novel titles in classroom sets for a group reading activity.

## ▷ INTRODUCING THE FOCUS

It is important to introduce children to the author/illustrator and to as many of his books as possible. It helps if some of the activities are school-wide or involve all of those who will be participating in the author/illustrator visit. There are several ways to introduce the focus:

- Make a movie-style marquee featuring a poster-sized photo of the author/illustrator and biographical information.
- Ask a staff member or volunteer to dress as one of the most recognizable characters from one of the author's/illustrator's books and read the book that features the character or give a short synopsis, encouraging listeners to read the book.
- Choose one of the author's/illustrator's books to read to all the classes or story hour participants. Share information about the author/illustrator and discuss how that person began to write or illustrate. Booktalk the artist's other books.
- Ask the art teacher or other resource person to help introduce the books by discussing any art elements in the books (especially in picture books).
- Write letters to the author/illustrator introducing your school or city. Include historical information about the community and the school.
- Set up a display of the author's/illustrator's books.
- Share information about the author/illustrator and then as a group create a book, "Ten Things I Know about (name of author)."
- Create an author/illustrator corner in your classroom or library media center.
- If a videotape of the author/illustrator or her works is available, incorporate it into your introduction.

You can combine and implement these suggestions in any number of ways. For example, when preparing for the school visit by Beatrice Schenk de Regniers, each classroom created an author's corner using a picture of the author and color copies of selected book jackets. The staff designated one week for introducing the author to our students, using a bulletin board display and a discussion of her life. They introduced the story line of *Little Sister and the Month Brothers* (Clarion, 1976) through one of two films, *The Twelve Months* (Journal Films, 1981) or *Twelve Months* (Coronet, 1980).

Following this introduction, they read the book aloud, discussed the story, and performed critical reading activities, comparing and contrasting the book and the film. The teachers introduced the idea of folk literature evolving as stories and shared a second book version of the story, *The Month Brothers: A Slavic Tale* retold by Samuel Marshak and translated by Thomas P. Whitney (Morrow, 1983).

From this starting point, each teacher selected other books to share and brought together activities and books to achieve goals and objectives that they and their classes had set. In each of the classrooms, the author focus spun off in different directions. Some emphasized the folklore aspect of de Regniers's, titles and connected her *Little Sister and the Month Brothers* to a Czech unit taught as an enrichment unit in our school. The art teacher incorporated a study of Henri Matisse and his paper collages with the theme suggested by de Regniers' circus title. Others created writing innovations based on *A Little House of My Own*. And several classrooms explored giant stories after reading de Regniers' version of *Jack and the Beanstalk*.

One classroom fashioned banners to welcome the author. Another made buttons to be worn by teachers, custodians, and cafeteria workers—each proclaiming that *Beatrice Schenk de Regniers Is Coming*. Table tents on cafeteria tables advertised the author's books, and her books were displayed in many author corners in both the library media center and individual classrooms. The entire school became focused on the visiting author and her books.

## ▶ GETTING READY IN OTHER SETTINGS

An introduction to author events to be held in public libraries will take some modification to the introductory activities used in schools. For example, a bulletin board or corner of the children's section of the library or a central area often seen by parents could become an author corner announcing the impending visit with a marquee-style poster. Information about the author/illustrator could be printed in the newsletter the library distributes to the public. Flyers giving the same information could be available at the circulation desk. Story hour sessions would feature books by the author/illustrator, and parents would be encouraged to check out books by the author/illustrator. If a video about the author is available, a special showing could be scheduled. (See "Videos About Authors and Illustrators" in Section 9, page 108-133.)

Organizations attempting to acquaint adults with the work of a specific author/illustrator could use some of the same techniques. Promotion will be the main thrust in these situations.

---

### DIANE STANLEY
**Leonardo Da Vinci**
**Shaka: King of the Zulus**
**A Time Apart**
**Rumpelstiltskin's Daughter**
**The Month Brothers: A Slavic Tale (Illustrator)**

Diane Stanley's illustrations for the Marshak tale depicted the month brothers more elaborately. Diane Stanley began illustrating children's books when in 1976 she asked herself, "What would you do if you could do it for a year?" Her response was to be a children's book illustrator. A year later she had put together a portfolio and submitted it to an editor at Little, Brown.

She began to illustrate various books, but it was much later before anyone would accept a text from her. It was also several years before anyone would accept the translated text for a Bohemian folktale, *The Month Brothers*. When the text was accepted, Stanley began to work on the illustrations, using a watercolor technique. After the initial watercolor was dry, she came back with a triple 000 brush to build up details (dry brush painting). She has created art for other books with colored pencils or gouache on parchment paper using marbleized borders.

Sometimes she writes the texts with her husband, Peter Vennema, and sometimes with her mother. Vennema and Stanley live in Houston, Texas, and often travel to research details to give authenticity to her illustrations. Being an artist—creating illustrations for children's books—is the thing Diane Stanley likes doing best.

After she had published picture books and several picture biographies, Stanley's first novel was published. That book, *A Time Apart* (William Morrow, 1999), debuted to rave reviews, as did her picture book biographies of Leonard da Vinci (William Morrow, 1997) and Michelangelo (William Morrow, 2000).

Stanley often makes visits to schools. You can find more information about whom to contact on her Web site at <http://www.dianestanley.com>. Diane Stanley is the recipient of the 2000 Washington Post/Children's Book Guild Nonfiction Award for the body of her work.

"I hope to drop over my drawing board at age 85."
— Diane Stanley

### ASHLEY BRYAN
*What a Wonderful World*
*All Day, All Night*
*The Dancing Granny*

When Ashley Bryan leaves his home to visit schools, he must take a ferry from his island home off the coast of Maine to the mainland. He has visited Africa several times and often travels across the United States to share his stories and poems. Sometimes he tells stories from his own books, such as "Ananse the Spider in Search of a Fool" in *The Ox of the Wonderful Horns* (Atheneum, 1971). But most often he begins by reciting poems by Langston Hughes, Paul Dunbar, Gwendolyn Brooks, and Eloise Greenfield. His presentation style invites participation. In one school, the entire student body of K-3 students had learned some of the spirituals he collected and illustrated in *All Day, All Night* (McElderry, 1991). Later some of the children joined in reciting some of the poems he was sharing with them. They particularly enjoyed the stanzas from poems in *Ashley Bryan's ABC of African American Poetry* (Atheneum, 1997).

"Poems bring you into the heart of a feeling. When I recite a poem, I always hold the book. Whatever the voice does it *lives in a book*."

—Ashley Bryan

## ▶ USING VIDEOS AND BOOKS ABOUT AUTHORS/ILLUSTRATORS

Sometimes videotapes or books about the author are available that can help to familiarize the children and adults with the featured author/illustrator and answer basic questions like "Where did the author get the information?" and "Did the story really happen?"

Author information is important to share for a number of reasons. It makes readers aware that those who write are people just like them. Writers and artists have some of the same problems and concerns as they do, some of the same successes and occasional failures. Readers expect writers of information books to do research, but few realize that even writers of fiction must verify facts so that their writing is credible. Learning about the writers' research efforts can inspire readers to evaluate the accuracy of the information contained in a book. Writers who include bits and pieces of their lives in their own writing (and most of them do) can help young readers understand traditions that differ from their own, understand people with a variety of goals and aspirations, and understand those people who grow up in a different culture from our own.

Some may question if knowing too much about an author/illustrator ahead of time will diminish enthusiasm for the actual visit and leave nothing for the author or illustrator to speak about. That was a concern to author Jacqueline Briggs Martin when, shortly before she visited a school, she learned that the children had viewed the video *Celebrating Authors: Meet Jacqueline Briggs Martin*. (Hi Willow, 1992). On the tape, Martin shares memories of her childhood on a farm and experiences with her own children that figure into her books. Filmed during a school visit, Martin describes the origins of some of the ideas that fuel her writing. She speaks of her son's fear of the wind that grew into her first book, *Bizzy Bones and Uncle Ezra*, (Lothrop, Lee, & Shepard Books, 1984) and sequels that incorporate episodes from a family camping trip and her daughter's French horn playing. In response to questions from the students, she shows her work in various stages of completion and acknowledges the time and effort it takes to write.

Knowing that this audience had viewed the tape, Martin found that she could talk about her new projects and give added information that built on the information she had found herself repeating visit after visit. Children were able to ask follow-up questions to some of the questions asked on the video. Martin could respond by referring to both the information she gave them that day as well as to the information shared on the video. She was pleased with the day, and the children were excited to be able to learn about her newest projects and what had inspired them.

Even though we used a video to introduce Martin to young readers, you could accomplish the same thing though a thorough study of the author's or illustrator's work. A thorough knowledge of the visiting author will only enhance her ability to relate to the audience.

Most authors emphasize that writing is a process of writing, revising, rewriting, revising, and more rewriting. Illustrators show the immense planning and energy that goes into each piece of artwork. Both encourage young writers to view their own life experiences, either personal or cultural, as potential topics for writing or illustrating. Those who write and illustrate children's books display their power of observation with everyday objects and incidents. On video, an author's or illustrator's story can also graphically illustrate the interrelation between other artistic endeavors and the creation of a book. For example, Ashley Bryan performs musically, Jack Prelutsky sings his poetry, and the late James Marshall played his fiddle.

## Authors on Video

In the early 1990s, many video companies used the medium to advantage to introduce young readers to writers and illustrators. One company, American School Publishers, seemed to hold the majority of the market when it came to author videos. They produced videos featuring Cynthia Rylant, Laura Ingalls Wilder, Mildred D. Taylor, Jack Prelutsky, Jerry Pinkney, and a host of other popular authors and illustrators. The quality of its videos was unsurpassed. With a few exceptions it seems to have targeted the audience compatible with the age of the audience for books. Regrettably, American School Publishers eventually went out of business. For a time, its products were distributed by SRA/McGraw-Hill. Then the line disappeared. A few of its videos are still available through such distributors as AIMS or Learning Video, but their catalogs and Web sites rarely list the actual producer, so it is difficult to figure out if the video is the original American School Publishers production.

Houghton Mifflin Publishers entered the field with videos featuring its published authors, such as Bill Peet, Russell Freedman, and Marvin Terban. In all, Houghton Mifflin had seven videos on its authors. The videos were, at the time, very up-to-date and did a great job focusing on the young audience that would be viewing the videos. In A *Visit with Bernard Waber*, young readers were given a tour of East 88th Street, the setting for the first Lyle, Lyle Crocodile tale.

On a video produced by Harcourt Brace, *Get to Know Bernard Most*, the author greeted viewers in his family's Scarsdale, New York home and discussed the research he must do to create his titles about dinosaurs.

Viewers of *A Visit with Eve Bunting* share some of Bunting's experiences as an Irish schoolgirl during Germany's bombings of World War II. Her days at a boarding school, her girlhood days in Ireland, and her immigration to the United States all appear in the writing she does today.

---

### BERNARD MOST
*Four & Twenty Dinosaurs*
*Whatever Happened to the Dinosaurs?*
*ABC T-Rex*

From the time he was in college, Bernard Most wanted to have a book of his published. When one of his young sons became interested in dinosaurs, so did Bernard. Now his sons, Eric and Glen, are grown, but Most is still writing about dinosaurs and other creatures.

When Most visits schools, the message he tries to give is "Don't get discouraged! Don't give up your ideas, goals, or dreams! Persistence, hard work, genuine love for what you are doing, and a lot of patience will make it happen."

— Bernard Most

Most's first book was published in 1980. His ninth book, *The Littlest Dinosaur*, was published by Harcourt in 1989—nine books in nine years. In the year 2000, Most had published 20 more titles. Although the Harcourt video about Most is no longer readily available, those who want to know more about him may wish to visit Harcourt's Web site at <http://www.bernardmost.com>. The site has a great interview with Bernard Most. The interviewer is his now grown son Eric.

### Eric Carle
*The Very Hungry Caterpillar*
*Walter the Baker*
*The Mixed-Up Chameleon*
*Dream Snow*

*The Mixed-Up Chameleon* (HarperCollins, 1975, 1987) title was inspired, in part, by the animals that Carle drew as he talked to children during school visits. Carle no longer makes school visits, but he does occasionally attend large gatherings, such as the American Library Association's annual conference. Most public speaking he does now is to adults. He speaks of his technique of making colored papers and the planning involved in writing and illustrating a book. He talks of the inspiration for much of his writing—his early years in the United States, his childhood in Germany during World War II, his return to the United States. At times he recounts the role Leo Lionni played in his career and his first association with Bill Martin, Jr., who asked Carle to illustrate his *Brown Bear, Brown Bear, What Do You See?* (Holt, Rinehart, 1967) after seeing Carle's art on a lobster advertisement. A revised edition of *Brown Bear* (H. Holt, 1992) showcases new illustrations Carle created with painted tissue papers instead of the commercial papers he used for earlier books. Carle's Web site at <http://www.eric-carle.com> contains information about his current publications, the Eric Carle Museum of Picture Book Art, funded by the Eric and Barbara Carle Foundation, and a page for sharing teacher ideas for using his books in the classroom.

Occasionally a company that does not normally produce videos produces one and makes it available to the public. *Celebrating Authors: Meet Carol Gorman* (1992) and *Celebrating Authors: Meet Jacqueline Briggs Martin* (1992) resulted directly from school visits. The video for a time was distributed by Hi Willow Research and Publishing. While no longer readily available, the video may be found in some libraries, particularly regional educational libraries serving individual schools or school districts. Carol Gorman's books had won several awards before the video was made and became even more popular when her *Dork in Disguise* (HarperCollins, 1999) was published.

Jacqueline Briggs Martin's video does a good job of dealing with her early career. She has become a popular author and among her most popular titles is the Caldecott Award book, *Snowflake Bentley*.

Coronet/MTI Films & Video is another company that distributed a video, *The Writing Process: A Conversation with Mavis Jukes*, produced by Walt Disney. Coronet/MTI Films & Video is no longer listed on the National Information Center for Educational Media (NICEM) site at <http://www.nicem.com>. Ishtar Films, another producer that seems to have disappeared, produced just one title, *Madeleine L'Engle: Star\*Gazer*. Both of these titles are excellent and worth checking libraries for.

In 1994, a relative newcomer to the video market was Tom Podell Productions. Podell has since gone on to create several dozen videos about authors/illustrators and at this time seems to be the only producer currently making informational videos about contemporary book creators. His earlier titles about such writers as Karla Kuskin or M. E. Kerr seemed uninspired, but because so little was available about some writers, they served a useful purpose, if only for selected segments. One of his titles, *Good Conversation! A Talk with Jean Craighead George* (1989), provided a tour of her interesting home. Even though the questions seem repetitive and poorly worded, viewers will enjoy George's animated personality, her family, and her home, where she displays many of her travel keepsakes. According to Tom Podell Production's Web site at <http://www.goodconversations.com>, the George video now carries a 1991 copyright date, which indicates it has been updated.

In recent years, Tom Podell has taped interviews with a number of authors of interest to young readers. For example, Christopher Paul Curtis (2000), whose *Bud, Not Buddy* (Delacorte, 1999) is enormously popular, is an interesting person. Podell has matured as an interviewer and so have his videos, which now are among some of the best available.

At times, publishers produce videos on their popular authors, often ones who no longer routinely make school visits. One such video is *Eric Carle: Picture Writer,* produced by Putnam & Grosset Book Group in cooperation with Scholastic, Inc. Viewers are treated to a look at Eric Carle's spacious studio, where he demonstrates how he makes the painted tissue papers he uses in his collages. He reads several of his books and explains the origins of others. Eric Carle no longer makes school visits, but he sometimes appears at conferences and workshops for adults. For those organizations, this tape will be a valuable addition to any focus on his work.

Some of the videos seem readily available only from video distributors such as AIMS and Library Videos.

### ▶ BOOKS ABOUT AUTHORS AND ILLUSTRATORS

Several books are available about authors and illustrators. Julian Messner, Inc. has published writer autobiographies—*The Moon and I* by Betsy Byars (1992), *Anonymously Yours* by Richard Peck (1992), and *The Invisible Thread* by Yoshiko Uchida (1992) are the first three—aimed at intermediate readers and usable also as background for younger readers. Byars and Peck sometimes appear at author events. Uchida died in 1992.

Richard C. Owen Publishers, Inc. produces another autobiographical series for younger readers, the *Meet the Author* collection. The first six titles in the series are *A Storyteller's Story* by Rafé Martin (1992), *Best Wishes* by Cynthia Rylant (1992), *A Bookworm Who Hatched* by Verna Aardema (1992), *Surprising Myself* by Jean Fritz (1992), *The Writing Bug* by Lee Bennett Hopkins (1993), and *A Letter from Phoenix Farm* by Jane Yolen (1993). Each gives young readers a glimpse into the authors' lives.

### LEE BENNETT HOPKINS
*The Writing Bug*
*My America: A Poetry Atlas of the United States*
*Good Books, Good Times!*
*Mama*

Both poet and anthologist, Hopkins has collected hundreds of poems in thematic anthologies. He has written two novels loosely based on his early life and has contributed teaching ideas that have been published in many periodicals. His enthusiasm for teaching and writing started in the early 1960s when he began to teach in New Jersey. He later became part of the resource team at the Bank Street School of Education and then an editor with Scholastic before turning to a full-time career as a writer. He often appears at conferences and conventions where his sessions focus on poetry. For the past 20 years or more, Hopkins has lived in the country overlooking the Hudson River in Scarborough, New York. A 1978 publicity brochure quotes him as saying, "When the writing bug stings you, the bite never heals"—a quote, it seems, that echoes the title for his autobiography. He demonstrated his generosity and commitment to promoting poetry by establishing the Promising Poet Award given every three years through the International Reading Association.

Martin discusses the connection between his storytelling and his writing. Rylant tells about her early years in Appalachia, where her grandfather was a coal miner and where many of her stories originate. Hopkins tells about his less-than-idyllic youth and his emergence as a teacher "bitten by the writing bug."

Obviously autobiographies can be only as accurate as the writer makes them and cover only events while the writer was living. In her autobiography, Verna Aardema introduces her family, who inspired her search for stories. Aardema died in 2000. Jean Fritz, the author of meticulously researched biographies, mentions vacation trips to the Caribbean Island Virgin Gored with her family. But those trips are now only pleasant memories, due to a back injury that has severely limited her mobility. Cynthia Rylant's book has her still living in Ohio, but she has since moved to Oregon and lives just down the road from her friend and fellow writer, Dav Pilkey.

## FAITH RINGGOLD
*Tar Beach*
*Aunt Harriet's Underground Railroad in the Sky*
*If a Bus Could Talk: The Story of Rosa Parks*
*My Grandmother's Story Quilt*

Sometimes books about authors and illustrators show up in unexpected places. For example, the series *Portraits of Women Artists for Children* by Robyn Montana Turner includes *Faith Ringgold* (Little, Brown, 1993). Turner's focus is on Ringgold's art, but her art is the direct inspiration for her books, including *Tar Beach* (Crown, 1991) and *Aunt Harriet's Underground Railroad in the Sky* (Crown, 1992)—books begun as stories told on quilts. The quilts are Ringgold's art, and Turner's story gives young readers insight into both quilting and storytelling.

## BYRD BAYLOR
*One Small Blue Bead*
*Moon Song*
*I'm in Charge of Celebrations*

"I read a lot as a child. I also lied a lot. I still read a lot. When I was eight or nine years old, I wrote a lot sitting on a hillside. I put the stories in a cigar box. Now I live in Arizona in the southern part by Mexico, eight miles from a little town. The road is so bad that it takes 30 minutes to get there. My adobe house is one big room. I couldn't stand putting walls in. I liked the space. I did put the bathroom in the greenhouse. The house has no electricity and no telephone. My writing is done with pencil and paper. I don't like the sound of mechanical things, and I write so slowly it would be an insult to a word processor."

— Byrd Baylor

Each of the writers discusses the sources for his inspiration, his writing schedule (or lack thereof), and the writing process. Full-color photographs on most of the pages lend a realistic note. Richard C. Own titles now include books about James Howe, Karla Kuskin, Paul Goble, Patricia Polacco, Lois Ehlert, Johanna Hurwitz, Patricia McKissack, and Seymour Simon. Not all of these authors/illustrators are available for school visits, but other types of author events may be possible.

Of course, the touchstone for autobiographies in the field of children's authors and illustrators is probably Bill Peet's Caldecott honor title, *Bill Peet: An Autobiography* (Houghton, 1989), in which Peet tells his life story, including his years with the Walt Disney Studios and his eventual emergence as a full-time author and illustrator of children's books. Because of throat cancer, Peet no longer makes personal appearances.

Faith Ringgold has been a popular conference speaker, sharing background about her art and writing that teachers can use to promote and motivate art projects and storytelling in both the classroom and at home.

I came across one unexpected find in a title for intermediate readers, *Famous Asian Americans* by Janet Nomura Morey and Wendy Dunn (Cobblehill, 1992), a collection of biographies of 14 prominent Asian Americans. One of the subjects is children's author and illustrator José Aruego, a native of the Philippines and a classmate and good friend of Benigno Aquino. Aquino was assassinated in 1983. His widow, Corazon Aquino, succeeded him as president of the Philippines and served until 1986. Aruego studied law and earned a law degree but abandoned his legal practice after just three months and came to the United States to study art at Parsons School of Design in New York. He has been in New York ever since and is now a U. S. citizen and a popular illustrator of children's books, including Robert Kraus's *Leo the Late Bloomer* (Windmill, 1971; Simon & Schuster, 1987) and *Milton the Early Riser* (Simon & Schuster, 1987).

Others have published collected interviews with several authors/illustrators. Pat Cummings, an author herself, has interviewed a number of other artists and included them in three *Talking with Artists* volumes. Leonard S. Marcus and Judy Blume edited a book of author interviews.

Libraries Unlimited's *100 Most Popular...* series contains biographies of authors and illustrators who are subjects of many author focus activities in schools and libraries. These one-volume biographies are appropriate for both adults and young readers.

In addition to titles written especially for young readers, several multi-volume adult reference works are available, including the *Something About the Author* series published by Gale Research, Inc. and the *Junior Books of Authors and Illustrators* series published by H. W. Wilson Company. Few of these references include large photos. They are written for adults, not for young readers. Two sources that do have photos and *are* addressed to schoolchildren are the *Author a Month* and the *Bookpeople* series from Libraries Unlimited. Though out of print, these titles may be available in many libraries.

*An Author a Month for Dimes* (Libraries Unlimited/TIP, 1992) has information about Byrd Baylor, a popular convention presenter. Many people assume that she is Native American, but those who meet her in person realize she is not, although she has the respect for animals, plants, and nature often attributed to Native Americans.

Linworth Publishing has collected over 21 interviews previously published in *Library Talk* or in *The Book Report* in *The Book Report & Library Talk Author Profile Collection* (1992). The interviews are with such people as Avi, Gail E. Haley, John Steptoe, David Wiesner, and Walter Dean Myers. In addition, Linworth's *Elementary Author/Illustrator Profiles* (1996) contains 32 of the profiles that are a regular feature of *Library Talk* and *The Book Report*. Since those collections, Linworth's journals have profiled Nicole Rubel, Louis Sachar, James Ransome, Nancy Werlin, Franny Billingsley, and Deborah Hopkinson, among others.

### DAVID WIESNER
*Tuesday*
*June 29, 1999*
*Hurricane*

"Every since I was a child I wanted to be an artist. It was the thing I loved doing best."
— David Wiesner (1992)

*Tuesday* (Clarion, 1991) came about when Wiesner wrote a story to accompany an illustration of a frog on a lily pad for the cover of *Cricket* (March 1987). In *Tuesday*, the flying frogs turn an ordinary Tuesday into an inspired adventure. Wiesner won the 1992 Caldecott award for the illustrations in that book. Some of his other books are *Hurricane* (Clarion, 1990), *Free Fall* (Lothrop, 1988), and *June 29, 1999* (Clarion, 1992). Wiesner and his surgeon wife, Kim Kahn, collaborated on *The Loathsome Dragon* (Putnam, 1987). After living for a number of years in New York and Philadelphia, they now live with their two sons, Kevin and Jaime, in the Midwest.

Other periodical sources, such as *Booklinks*, which deals with books for thematic units, and *Booklist*, a professional reviewing source, often include author interviews. Both are published by the American Library Association. Locate author interviews in these and other sources by using *Biography Index*, an H. W. Wilson reference that indexes articles, books, and chapters of books that contain biographical information about notable figures in all walks of life, including children's book publishing. (See "Books About Authors and Illustrators" in Section 9, page 113-114.)

## ▶ AUTHOR AND ILLUSTRATOR WEB SITES AS A RESOURCE

Where once we used filmstrips, cassettes, and videotapes to introduce authors and illustrators to students, we now can turn to the World Wide Web to find information as well as pictures and even video clips. Most sites have biographical information about the authors/illustrators and lists of their books. The best sites offer visitors something more than a "sales pitch" for their books or for author visits. Some authors' Web sites are elaborate, but some of the most elaborate are not well designed.

One of the first questions I ask is whether or not the creator of the Web site has accurately recognized the site's audience. Some sites are intended for children to access and learn about a favorite author; on the other end of the continuum are sites designed for adults working with children. Others are somewhere in between. Probably most popular are sites that offer the educator ideas for extending the books and perhaps even lesson plans and pages that appeal to young readers as well.

One of the best of these types is Jan Brett's site at <http://www.janbrett.com>. Her pages have information for educators plus pages where children can enter contests, send postcards, or learn more about characters in her books. Often there are illustrations to print. At times, she has included puppet faces or other dramatic aids with permission to print and use them in the classroom. Teachers enjoy the ideas, and children enjoy the interactive contests and activities.

The creator of Tomie dePaola's site works for dePaola but says the site is not "official" in that it is not maintained by the author himself nor by the author's publisher. In fact, he says, the site is actually that of a fan. It carries information about dePaola's books—what new ones are in the planning stages, where one can purchase autographed copies—and anecdotal information about the author. It is useful to teachers though it does not have suggestions for using the books but concentrates instead on information that can help teachers decide what books to use.

Jane Kurtz's site at <http://www.janekurtz.com> provides background on each of her books, reviews and curriculum connection suggestions, and links to related information. Teachers can share the information with students; those reading Kurtz's *The Storyteller's Beads* can find background information that will enhance their reading. Readers of her picture books will find information about games and objects mentioned in them.

Other sites are intended to let visitors know what books the authors have written and published. These pages are useful as a bibliographic resource, but the same information can be obtained from an online book dealer such as Barnes and Noble (<http://www.bn.com>) or Amazon.com (<http://www.amazon.com>). (The author's site won't, however, carry the heavy advertising ever present on commercial sites.)

Know the limits of the site before you assume that it can be used for children. Just because an author's/illustrator's books are written for children does not mean that his Web site will be intended for them.

A second element that I view as very important is the overall design of the page. I don't want it cluttered with links embedded in image maps that do not allow you to enlarge text. Frames sometimes make a site too cumbersome for efficient use in a school setting. Graphics must be worth the time to load and view. Especially irritating are sites created on a large monitor that have set widths controlled by the coding. Those of us with narrower monitors (15 inches, for example) must constantly scroll from left to right to see all the information.

The very best way to determine if a site is worth using in the classroom is to preview it thoroughly before attempting to share it with student users.

## *Authors and Illustrators on the Web*

Web sites can often provide information not readily available in print. If a Web site is regularly updated, visitors can find out about just-released books as well as forthcoming titles. But some sites are not updated regularly. For example, E. B. Lewis, one of my favorite authors, has a Web site (<www.eblewis.com>) that on my last visit listed four titles as "forthcoming" that had already been published. Obviously this site was no more valuable than a printed resource. But sites often have information that is too current to be found in books or other publications or that may not be as interesting in another format.

Janet Stevens's Web site (<http://www.janetstevens.com>) tells how she used digital tools to help create art for a book, *Cook-a-Doodle-Doo!* (Harcourt Brace, 1999), she co-authored with her sister, Susan Stevens Crummel. Don Wood uses his pages on Audrey Wood's Web site to tell how he uses technology to illustrate his books, including *Jubal's Wish* (Blue Sky Press, 2000). A picture on the Web shows his computer and stylus. The possibilities seem endless.

Deborah Hopkinson's site (<http://people.whitman.edu/~hopkinda/>) is a teacher's dream—quick to load, clear, and easy to access. She has links to many other sites that connect with her many books about the Underground Railroad, Fannie Farmer, and Fisk University's Jubilee Singers. Zero in on a book and you'll find ideas to connect it to every area of the curriculum. Hopkinson maintains her own Web site and answers e-mail. Classes can arrange to communicate with her as a class activity.

Betsy Byars does not have an e-mail address but does have a Web site at <http://www.betsybyars.com> and provides her U.S. mail address so visitors can write to her. An added attraction is pictures of two other children's book writers, her daughters Betsy Duffey and Laurie Myers.

Authors' Web sites often have nuggets of information found nowhere else. Some have the writer or artist's e-mail or mailing address. Others, such as Tomie dePaola's "unofficial site" (<http://www.tomiedepaola.com>), provide no direct connection. (dePaola receives about 10,000 letters a month—many more than he can possibly answer. Even if he could, the postage would cost him $3,400 a month or $40,800 a year!)

More and more authors and illustrators are promoting themselves on the Web instead of waiting for someone to feature them in a book. The World Wide Web has opened up the world of self-promotion, and many authors and illustrators are taking advantage of it. Many have established domain names (sites that reflect their name, such as <http://www.janetstevens.com>, <http://www.betsybyars.com>, and <http://www.jacquelinebriggsmartin.com>). A list of many of my favorite author/illustrator sites, along with some gateways to author/illustrator sites, can be found in Section 9.

## *One Connection for 25 or More Students*

You can use an author's/illustrator's Web site effectively for groups of children. Having one Internet connection for an entire classroom need not be a deterrent to introducing authors/illustrators via the Web. You will need a large-screen projector to display the images on your computer monitor. This can be a large monitor through which you can display the computer images or an LCD panel or projector. Before bringing the Web site up on the large screen, enlarge the font size to 18- or 24-point so everyone can see it. (One reason image maps aren't effective in the classroom is that text in an image is part of the graphic and can't be enlarged, unlike text that appears on the screen as text.)

After you've demonstrated how to move through the Web site, you may want to give students a chance to explore it on their own. For example, those who have read *The True Confessions of Charlotte Doyle* (Orchard Books, 1990) can locate more historical fiction by Avi. Going to his site at <http://www.avi-writer.com>, they'll find an icon that takes them to a list of Avi's books in that genre. Each title is linked to a fact about the book. For example, the page featuring *The True Confessions of Charlotte Doyle* tells about connections between that book and a previous one, *The Man Who Was Poe* (Orchard, 1989), and challenges visitors to find the references in *Charlotte Doyle*. After individual students visit the connection throughout the day, let them discuss with the class what each learned about Avi's books.

Similar activities can involve demonstrating Jan Brett's site and allowing each child to send a postcard to someone special. Those visiting Jim Aylesworth's site can learn about his books and click on his e-mail link to send him a comment about his books. You'll get ideas for other activities as you visit other author and illustrator sites that interest you and your students.

## *Researching and Sharing the Information*

Author/illustrator Web sites are often most valuable for the information you can research and share with classes. For example, on the Avi site mentioned above, you could share the information about the connection between *The True Confession of Charlotte Doyle* and *The Man Who Would Be Poe* with a group reading the novel and challenge them to find the connections. Other information on the author's Web site could lead to other activities.

Children will enjoy hearing what Jane Kurtz says on her Web site about her childhood in Ethiopia and the basis for some of her stories. The students may derive a deeper understanding of the stories themselves. Showing the class how to maneuver through the site can help individuals use it when they have time to actually read and assimilate the information.

For example, the Web page for the book *Trouble* (Gulliver, 1997) mentions the game of gebeta and contains links to the family of games that includes gebeta. Children can learn about the game's rules and variations. Though the directions for the games might be too difficult for young readers, adults might use the instructions and the game pieces to teach children to play the game.

Author/illustrator sites are really no different from other sites. Before using one, preview it and decide whether the site is child-friendly enough to use directly with youngsters or if you would do better to use it as professional research to formulate activities and plans for sharing the author's/illustrator's books.

## ▶ READING MOTIVATION

An author focus does more than just encourage children to read one artist's books. It provides a structure for sharing literature and achieving curriculum and program goals through activities that relate to the author's/illustrator's work. The focus can teach students to respect the body of the author's/illustrator's work. As they read more and more of the author's/illustrator's books, they will see connections among them and use the library to seek out other books with connecting themes. Recognizing each new connection leads to a sense of achievement and challenges the reader to think in new terms. The more connections children discover, the more they will bring literature and books into their daily lives, across all subject levels. Children learn that their ideas and connections have validity and that each idea can lead to more connections and learning.

All of this is possible only if the author's/illustrator's books and many collaborative books for reading are available to children.

## SECTION 5

# Making the Day Shine

The value of advance planning for every detail cannot be emphasized enough. Each bit of advance planning will pay dividends in terms of a successful day. Whatever arrangements you can make in advance will reduce stress on the day itself. Specifically, plan for

- The schedule for the day itself,
- Welcoming activities, and
- Arrangements for the book sales and autographing sessions.

## ▶ SCHEDULING THE DAY

Formulate a schedule several weeks before the visit. In general, four presentations (40-60 minutes) are maximum for any one-day school visit. Each is simply too energy-consuming for more sessions to be effective. If an author is going to be in your area for several days under a cost-sharing arrangement, three presentations would be a more reasonable maximum. Educators sometimes do not recognize that being the center of attention for a full eight-hour or even six-hour day is much more taxing than being with a classroom of children with whom they have an established relationship.

An author/illustrator must come in, build rapport, provide inspiration, and leave everyone she meets with a positive feeling. There's no opportunity to redeem oneself the next day. Some authors/illustrators specify fewer than three or four sessions as the maximum. Whatever the agreement, respect it. Build in time to set up equipment, breaks for collecting thoughts and using the restroom, an appropriate lunch period, and autographing time. Distribute the schedule to staff early enough to allow any conflicts to be resolved.

Given the complexity of most school schedules—with physical education, music, and art classes as well as lunch and recesses—it is not always possible to meet all the requests of each teacher. Having those with an overall view of the whole situation create the schedule will give you the best chance of accommodating the most people.

## Sample Schedule

8:00 a.m. — Continental breakfast reception with staff

8:45 a.m. — Set up equipment; prepare for first session

9:05 a.m. — All-school assembly to introduce author/illustrator and welcome him with readings, key to school

9:30 a.m. — First session (fourth and fifth grades)—50 minutes with 10 minute break

10:30 a.m. — Second session (second and third grades)—50 minutes

11:20 a.m. — Lunch

12:30 p.m. — Third session (kindergarten and first grade)—40 minutes

1:10 p.m. — Break; if time, autographing of books left with autographing slips

1:30 p.m. — Classes visit the library to have their picture taken with the author/illustrator

3:00 p.m. — Final autographing in the library

Schedules for other types of author visits will be as varied as the events themselves. In the case of a workshop appearance for adults, the schedule might be informal with coffee and rolls, a break for collecting thoughts and using the restroom before the presentation, a 45- to 60-minute presentation that may extend a little longer for a question-and-answer session, and finally a time for autographing. It's the host's job to see that workshop participants do not detain the author/illustrator before the presentation and that the autographing session is not a personal forum for just a few overzealous admirers. Starting and stopping on time are essential.

One multi-day, multi-host author visit included school visits, an evening event for area educators and parents, and a public library-sponsored "conversation with the author/illustrator." The latter was an occasion for introducing the author/illustrator to the community. It began with coffee and rolls; participants had ample time to mingle and talk informally. After 30 to 45 minutes, the host introduced the author, and the group had an opportunity to ask questions. As with the other events, books were available for autographing, and the visit ended with an autographing session.

## Avoiding the Pitfalls

One of the errors that many schools make when scheduling an author visit is to allow too little transition time. It takes time to move groups of children in and out of a common room. It is a rare special event that does not necessitate some adjustment to the normal school day. Class periods may have to be lengthened to accommodate a longer session with the author. Teachers may find themselves having to alter their classroom schedules. Rather than attempting to satisfy everyone's special request, sit down with the school's master schedule and make a timetable that accounts for the presenter's needs as well as individual class schedules as much as possible.

Sometimes teachers have switched times that particular classes would come to them so that groups can attend the author's presentation. At other times, cafeteria workers have agreed to an extended lunch period so that a class could attend a presentation that extended into its normal lunchtime.

Probably the greatest pitfall in school visit schedules is not circulating the schedule early enough so that individuals can work out any snags unforeseen by the person who developed the schedule. Teachers are creative people; they can make the necessary adjustments if given ample time to do so.

Similar problems can occur during major conferences. One that will be obvious once it occurs is scheduling too short a time for breaks. If restroom facilities are inadequate, there will still be a line when the conference session resumes. At one conference of mostly women, both main restrooms were ladies' rooms; a small restroom in an office area was opened for the men, and the meeting stayed on schedule.

## ▶ OBTAINING BOOKS FOR AUTOGRAPHING SESSIONS

Part of the excitement of an author visit is being able to obtain an autographed book. Make arrangements at least three months prior to the author's visit. Let children and staff purchase books well in advance of the visit so there will be plenty of copies for reading and discussion. Personal copies of the books will help reduce the demand on library copies, especially during the final weeks before the visit.

Sending home book order forms will help you estimate the quantity to order as well as build anticipation for the visit. (See "Sample Book Order for an Author/Illustrator Visit"—Form 13 in Section 8, page 104.) Consult with the publisher about the lead time needed to receive the books at least two to three weeks before the author's visit. Using that date as a deadline, arrange to give booktalks to each class.

## *Do It Yourself, or "Contracting" the Book Sales*

You may obtain the books either directly from the publisher or through a local book distributor. Publishers usually offer the best discount. However, there are many details to deal with, including sending back unsold books and paying the postage if you over-estimate the number of books you'll need. Even though librarians are familiar with procedures necessary to order books, few deal directly with publishers or order multiple copies of titles, some of which may not be sold. Book dealers generally know the procedures for multiple buying and do the job more efficiently. The book dealer will work with you to select the available titles and estimate the number to order.

If you choose to order the books directly from the publisher, be sure to work with a liaison at the publishing house to ensure that you are given the "author visit" discount and that the books arrive in time for the author's visit. The publicist with whom you are working should be able to provide a contact person at the publishing house who will oversee your order. If, however, you choose to work with a book dealer, be sure to put all arrangements for discount, who is to pay return postage and so forth, in writing. The book dealer is often able to offer a 20 to 25 percent discount. If the number of titles ordered is a consensus decision between the dealer and the planning committee, it is not unusual for the book dealer to pay return postage for any unsold books or for you and the book dealer to share the cost.

As an incentive to order books ahead of time rather than wait until the day of the visit, you may wish to offer the books at the discounted price during the preorder process. On the day of the visit, they would cost the full retail price. This could generate a modest profit to pay for the return of any unsold books.

In schools, the actual sale of the books can be handled in a variety of ways. Two successful methods both include obtaining prepayment for books ordered; each involves sending home an order form. The most efficient method asks that the order blanks be returned to each classroom teacher; on the final due date, the teacher sends the forms and payments for the whole class to the library media center or designated book sale coordinator. The coordinator tallies the orders and verifies the payments. The combined order is made and the money deposited. Once the books arrive, they are distributed to the classroom with the original order form. The teacher makes the final distribution to students.

The other method is simply a variation of the first one. A similar form is used, but the orders are returned to a designated place in the school and each order is taken individually. The classroom teacher does not handle any part of the ordering procedure. When the books arrive, they are distributed from the same designated place. Most of this is handled by parent volunteers before and after the school day begins. This second method eliminates some teacher involvement, but it can become hectic since the volunteers deal with each student individually. The first method, which asks the teachers to collect the order slips, helps by grouping orders in lots. The sorting and delivery become much less involved, and the major part of the process can be handled by one person who collects and compiles the orders. Several volunteers are necessary if each order is taken directly from each child.

Regardless of the procedure you use to order and distribute the books, supply an autographing slip with each book that is delivered. (See Form 14 in Section 8, page 105.) A more complete discussion of the use of autographing slips is included in the discussion of autographing sessions.

Sales on the day of the visit or any time after the preorder deadline will need to be handled in a different manner. If books are available at the school before the visit, casual sales could be han-

### FRED BOWEN
*Winners Take All*
*T.J.'s Secret Pitch*
*The Golden Glove*

"Author visits show kids that there is a very real person behind the books they read. And, believe me, it's a surprise to some kids. I remember one mother telling me that her son treasured the book I signed for him at an author visit. Her son later showed the book to a friend and said proudly, 'See, the author signed it.' Instead of being impressed, his friend was confused and asked: 'You mean the author isn't dead?'"

—Fred Bowen

dled by clerical or volunteer help in the library media center. If the extra books will be at school only on the day of the visit, you will need to designate a place for sales. Have change and autographing slips on hand. Generally most of the books will sell in the first hour or so of the school day since children will arrive at school with the money for them.

When books are to be sold at other types of author/illustrator events, such as a public library appearance or children's literature conference, arrangements will be needed not only to sell the books but for the autographing sessions as well. Set up a "display only" table with a copy or two of each of the books available for purchase. Above the display table, post the titles and prices. As specific titles are sold out, cross them out on the poster. If the group attending is large, provide order slips and ask those wanting to buy books to fill out the order slip and take it to the order table. Personnel behind the table will fill the order and move the order down the table to the cashier to verify the total price and collect the payment. At this point, give the buyer an autographing slip for each title purchased. If the group is small, book sales can be handled more casually, much as they would be at a book fair.

Volunteers provide valuable assistance with book sales and autographing. If you have difficulty obtaining enough volunteers, however, you may wish to consider asking high school or college students to provide clerical assistance during large conferences or festivals. Or you might arrange for an organization such as the Thespian Club, French Club, or wrestling team—any group that wishes to raise money—to help. In return for your depositing a set amount ($200 to $300) in the club or organization's school account, the group would agree to supply 15 students at specified peak times during the conference and to keep no less than five students at the conference throughout the event. The planning committee would outline the students' duties, and an adult sponsor of the organization could supervise them. These young people may also enjoy hearing the speakers and will certainly project a positive image to those attending the event.

## ▶ MAKING THE GUEST OF HONOR WELCOME

One of the major goals of any author/illustrator school visit is to motivate reading and build a community of readers. The visit will be most effective if it is considered the culmination of a celebration. As the day draws closer, discuss the activities designed to officially welcome the guest of honor. Brainstorm ideas to add to the "welcoming" activities below:

- Hang a banner in the main foyer to welcome the author/illustrator.
- Mount posters in the halls advertising specific books by the author/illustrator.
- Make book tents for the lunchroom tables advertising books by the author/illustrator.
- Put up displays about the artist in classrooms, library, and hallways.
- Write a letter to the author/illustrator, including a map to the school or library.
- Create displays related to the author/illustrator.

If the event is a reception or informal function, find some way to identify the author/illustrator, such as a corsage or boutonniere. Nametags are also appropriate but harder to read from a distance. Hang welcoming banners and display

student art and writing as well as books by the author/illustrator.

Thematic decorations can add to the welcoming atmosphere of the presentation area. Auditoriums have been transformed into western frontiers, interiors of barns, or 18th-century scenes. Big red dogs would be fitting decorations for functions featuring Norman Bridwell, author of *Clifford, the Big Red Dog* (Scholastic, 1963). Jan Brett could be welcomed by large cutout figures of the many animal characters from her books or serenaded with Rimsky-Korsakov's "The Flight of the Bumblebee," as an element from *Berlioz the Bear* (Putnam, 1991). Or, since Brett has adopted the hedgehog as her unofficial mascot, perhaps that animal could provide the theme for decorations.

Our school invited an author of picture books, Jacqueline Briggs Martin, to meet the children in grades K-2 and an author of novels, Carol Gorman, to speak to grades 3-5. The visits were scheduled one week apart. Even though each author would be meeting only a portion of our student body, we felt that it was important that everyone be aware of the other author and present a total welcoming atmosphere on the day of each visit.

The idea of an author visiting was very much in the minds of all students. A bulletin board in the library featured poster-sized photos of each of the authors along with the dates each would be visiting. Books by both authors were displayed on the ledge below the bulletin board.

A week or two before Martin's visit, the library media specialist invited each of the third through fifth grade classrooms into the library media center and introduced them to Jacqueline Briggs Martin. She read one of Martin's books to them and shared information about the artist and her books. She showed the children a press sheet of one of Martin's books and discussed how a book gets published. But her main goal was to help students in the intermediate grades recognize the artist and respect her work. She asked each group to greet Martin if they saw her in the hallways or lunchroom and let her know how pleased we were to have her as a guest.

We held similar sessions with the primary classes to introduce them to Carol Gorman and her novels. We discussed what a novel is and how it differs from the books most of them were checking out of the library media center. The library media specialist read aloud a few pages of *T.J. and the Pirate Who Wouldn't Go Home* (Scholastic, 1990) and some of the teachers read the whole book to their classes.

One first grade class in particular loved the book. On the day of Gorman's visit, she was autographing a few books in the library before getting ready for her first session when a first grader appeared with a note from her first grade class. Arriving at school, she had peeked in the door of the library media center, recognized Carol Gorman, and raced to her classroom to proclaim "She's here, she's here."

The excitement was more than the teacher could handle. Requests to just go to the library to see her snowballed. Finally, in desperation, the teacher sent the first grader with a note from the group asking "Can we come down and just look at Carol Gorman?" The author readily agreed to being put on display, and the class came into the library media center, filed down one aisle of books, gave the author a friendly wave, circled down another aisle, and disappeared back to their room. They later wrote Gorman a thank-you note for letting them "stare at you." This teacher had done an excellent job of sharing the excitement of reading with her students. Now, several years later, those former first graders are fourth graders reading Gorman's novels for themselves. The excitement of that author visit has lasted for several years.

Many other types of promotional and welcoming activities might be part of the preparations for an author visit. Consider requesting the mayor of your city to proclaim the day or week in honor of the guest. Plan a ceremony to introduce the author/illustrator to the entire student body and present him with the key to the school or the city. Prepare and give the author/illustrator a proclamation honoring her as a VIG (Very Important Guest).

## ▶ WHAT QUESTIONS WILL YOU ASK?

Question-and-answer sessions are often included as part of a school visit. As you prepare for the visit, hold practice sessions (especially for primary grades) to help students formulate appropriate questions. Young students often have difficulty distinguishing between questions and comments. When they are given an opportunity to ask questions, they make a personal comment instead. Practice sessions will help them learn how to formulate questions. Discussions with older students should center on appropriate questions and listening.

### *Finding Out the Obvious Before the Visit*

Review with students what they know about the author/illustrator and discuss the types of questions to which they already know the answers, for example, "What books have you written?" or "Do you illustrate your books?" Basic information about the artist is generally included in the resource booklet. Share that information with students—facts such as titles and numbers of books written and basic biographical information. There are many sources where staff and students can learn about their prospective guest.

Search for relevant Web sites. Many authors' and illustrators' own sites are listed in Section 9, page 118-119 "Author/Illustrator Web Sites." However, a search using a Web search engine may yield additional sites with pertinent articles, interviews, or related information. The many resource books that may be of help are listed in "Books About Authors and Illustrators" in Section 9, page 113-114.

### *A Few Guidelines*

In discussing question-and-answer sessions, remind students to

- Listen to questions as well as answers to avoid repeating questions or asking things that have already been answered as part of another question.

- Think about information that we already know about the author/illustrator and her work and ask questions based on what you know. For example, not all writers illustrate their own books, and not all illustrators write. Ask questions such as "How long did it take you to draw the illustrations?" only of the illustrator.

- Put their hands down when the guest artist or a classmate is speaking.

- Remember that others will want to ask questions too. Once you've asked a question, don't monopolize the session.
- Be polite. Some questions many feel are impolite to ask of anyone, including two standouts: "How old are you?" and "How much money do you make?"

---

**LYNN HALL**
*Danza*
*Half the Battle*
*Dagmar Schultz and the Green-Eyed Monster*

"Whenever I am asked how much money I make, I always tell them, 'I make as much money as I spend.'"
— Lynn Hall

---

## ▶ OPPORTUNITIES TO PROMOTE READING AND YOUR SCHOOL OR ORGANIZATION

Several weeks in advance, distribute information about the author's/illustrator's visit to television stations and newspapers. Write a cover letter in the form of a news release. Make sure the release has some newsworthy information, such as an opportunity for parents and members of the community to visit an in-school presentation or a special event planned in honor of the author/illustrator. In the package, include basic information about the author/illustrator. List a name and phone number for newspeople to contact for additional information. Personally contact the education reporter or book page editor of the local newspaper to offer to arrange an interview.

If the newspaper does not send a photographer or wish to interview the author/illustrator, take some quality pictures of your own and write an article about the visit. Submit it to the newspaper. The editor may use it, especially if the photos show something of interest, not merely children posing with the author/illustrator, and the article conveys the personal aspect of the visit. Use quotes; emphasize information that will interest a general readership. Develop an angle that makes the author/illustrator unusual and interesting. For example, when attempting to interest our Iowa media in Colorado author/illustrator Craig McFarland Brown, we mentioned his Iowa connection; he spent his childhood in a town just 50 miles west of our city. David Wisniewski's experience as a circus clown made good copy and gave the media a hook to hang the story on.

Write an article for your school newsletter, inviting interested parents to attend the presentations. Ask children to write reviews of the author's/illustrator's books. Mention an opportunity for parents to purchase copies of the books.

## ▶ PHOTOGRAPHING THE DAY'S ACTIVITIES

If you want photos of the day's events, plan for them in advance. Ask a talented parent or student to be the official photographer. Many photographers' favorite is a 35mm camera with a long lens and high-speed color print film (1600 ASA/ISO). The high-speed film allows photographs to be taken in a variety of indoor settings even if the lighting is not optimum. Some will want to use a digital camera, and that is certainly appropriate if the photos are going to be used for Web pages or incorporated into electronic presentations of some sort or another.

### *Keeping an Eye on the Objective*

Decide in advance why you want pictures taken. What will you be using them for? Will you be putting them on the school's Web site? If so, make sure to record the names of the children pictured in each photo so you can obtain permissions. Some schools have an ironclad guideline that prohibits placing any photos of present students on the school's Web site. Thus, if you are going to use the photos on your school Web site, be careful that you get the photo you want without recognizable children in the shot.

If you are going to take a group photo with the author/illustrator, one objective will be to make sure all students' faces are visible in the photo. There is a trick to doing that. It helps to have someone help set up class photos, someone who knows that lining up students by size, putting the tallest in the back and the shortest in front, is actually not the most efficient way to arrange a group. There may not be enough difference in their sizes; the tallest students' faces may be hidden by those almost the same height.

A system that seems to work better is to divide the class into three sections. The first third of students should be the tallest group (with the tallest two students in the middle); the second third should be the shortest students (again arranged so the tallest are in the middle); and the final third should be in-between in height. Have the tallest third stand as far back against the backdrop as possible with the middle (tallest) two students turning to face one another and the rest of the row also turning toward the middle, shoulders toward the camera. The second line (the shortest third of the class) stands in the same manner as the back row. Ask the final row (the in-betweens) to kneel or sit cross-legged on the floor and the visiting author and teacher to join one of the rows. The cameraperson should be able to see every face.

Be sure to photograph the author autographing books and giving his presentation, and take other candid shots. Again keep in mind the purpose for which you want the photos. You can take pictures of displays, welcoming banners, and posters before the author/illustrator arrives, perhaps even the day before the visit.

## Digital or Prints?

Many consider digital cameras to be a cost-saving method of capturing images of special events. Digital pictures of low resolution are fine for use on Web pages but are not of high enough quality to put in print publications of any sort. Photo shops can print the digitized photo on photo paper, but for a third more of the cost, you can buy a roll of high-speed 35 mm film (36 exposures) and get triple prints. You can digitize a print by scanning the image as a tif, gif or jpeg formatted image. If your school has a scanner, the scanned image will be free, and you will still have the hard copies for sharing with other staff members, sending to the author/illustrator, and using in a bulletin board display. Scanning a hard copy also lets you control the pixels per inch and thus create a high-resolution image suitable for newspaper or newsletter reproduction. Low-resolution graphics are generally appropriate only for Web or other electronic uses. Decide why you want the photo, and then make sure the shots will meet your needs—and that whoever is taking the photos knows your objectives and restrictions.

If the author/illustrator will be speaking in the same room for each presentation, provide an appropriate background for photos. If the presentations will take place in different rooms, decide in advance where the author/illustrator will stand so that the background will be suitable. The best background is often a display of the guest artist's books, posters of the books, or an appropriate bulletin board. Be careful that the background is not too cluttered. The composition of the photographs is important. Ask the photographer to concentrate on getting close-ups.

If there is time and if the author/illustrator agrees, take a picture of each class with the author. After the visit, offer copies of the photo, at cost, to the students in each class. Number each of the authors' photos, post them, and take orders. Some students may want copies of some of the other photos taken during the day. The bookkeeping (who ordered what) will be much more manageable if the ordering is done through classroom groups. Each teacher should take orders, collect payment, and submit a class order. When the copies are made, they can be distributed to the teacher who in turn distributes them to the students who ordered them.

## Video—Is It Worth It?

If you plan to videotape the event, obtain permission from the author/illustrator—before her arrival, not at the same time the camera is being set up with the assumption that she'll say yes. If you obtain permission in writing, by all means plan to videotape.

Keep in mind that few people will want to watch the entire day's proceedings on six hours or more of tape, so you will want to be selective or plan to edit the tape. Again, decide ahead of time why you want the video. If it is to show other classes, you might want to think about the wisdom of that. Often, unless you have a professional doing the videotaping, the quality of the film is not the quality that will keep the attention of a group seeing it secondhand. You will be too busy to operate the camera, so you'll have to rely on others to get the film you need. Don't sacrifice the success of the day just to have a tape of questionable quality.

## *Sharing the Photos*

Others may want copies of photos, especially class photos, taken during the author's/illustrator's visit. The easiest way to accommodate this is to mark a copy of each photograph with a negative number. Post the numbered photographs and let people order the ones they want, at the cost of having the copies made. Set a deadline and then submit the order. A simple page of notebook paper for each negative number (with payment in advance) will allow students and staff to sign up for each photo they want.

If you get duplicate prints made, consider sending a copy in your thank-you notes. Always plan on giving each teacher a copy of his class photo. If you had parent volunteers, attempt to get a candid shot of their child with the author/illustrator and see that they get a copy of it. For sure, manage to shoot a picture of the principal with the author/illustrator on that day. I'd even spring for a simple frame and mat to make sure she can set the picture on her desk. All of these gestures will cost a few dollars but will reap rewards far more valuable.

## ▶ PROVIDING A PERSONAL HOST

The author/illustrator often arrives in the community the day before the first scheduled school or library visit. A member of the planning committee should plan to meet him at the airport or point of arrival. Arrange to have an identifiable sign (perhaps a book the author/illustrator has created) to help the guest identify the hostess. If the arrival time is early enough, the author/illustrator may appreciate a dinner invitation with a couple of members of the committee. Be sure that the group isn't so large that the he feels as if this is another appearance. Dinner invitations for evenings the guest is in your locale may also be welcome; however, some visiting authors prefer to have time on their own to work on projects or plan their own agenda.

Make arrangements for the guest to be driven to the school or other site on the morning of the visit. If she has driven to your city or has a rental car and prefers to drive herself to the day's site, it still may be thoughtful to offer to send someone to escort her. Throughout the day, a host should be available to take the author/illustrator through the building, introduce her at each presentation, and bring each session to a close.

It is important to make beverages available throughout the day. Be prepared to offer ice water, hot or cold tea, coffee, or soft drinks. Especially during the presentations, have a pitcher of water and a glass near the speaker's podium. The host should also be part of any arrangements for lunch. You will have found out about any dietary restrictions or requests early in the planning.

If you hold a staff reception for the guest at the beginning or end of the day, the host should introduce each staff member and make sure that the visitor is able to visit with each of them a short time. It is gracious to personalize each introduction with a significant bit of information. Name tags are a help to most guests.

The host or hostess should be someone who is very familiar with the author's/illustrator's books and has a real interest in the visit. She should be free of other duties in order to devote her entire day to making the author/illustrator as comfortable as possible. In the case of school visits, it may be necessary to hire a substitute teacher to take over the hostess's regular duties.

The host will play a major part in making the day a memorable one for the staff and the students, as well as for the author/illustrator. A thoughtful host will cue the visitor in on facts about the children or participants as they arrive for presentations. For example, if the class created the hallway mural depicting a sequence of scenes from one of the artist's books, the host would mention this before the session with that class.

A hostess or host is especially important at adult events where some participants may be so intrigued with meeting the author/illustrator that they may monopolize the visitor's free time. The hostess will need to help the visitor circulate through the group. If participants are actually approaching the guests with their requests for autographing, she'll need to help move the autograph line along. One of her most important tasks may be to see that the guest has time to visit the restroom and get a drink of water and that he arrives at a luncheon on time. Be sure the host or hostess is someone who can handle this responsibility.

One local college invites an author annually to speak to its students. Elementary students are invited to the daytime presentations and the public to an evening presentation. One year the college department head was pressed into service as the host when the conference director fell ill. The department head handled the daytime sessions fairly well, but before the evening presentation he and a few other department people took the author out for dinner—a fine gesture except that an autographing session had been scheduled to start at 6:45 and the presentation at 7:30. The group arrived at the auditorium at 7:35, explaining that they "just got so interested in telling stories." All the while, 150 people were waiting.

To top it all off, the planners had not checked the slide projector's remote, and the first 20 minutes of the speaker's presentation were interrupted by "It's working," then "It's not working," until finally the problem was solved. Some things, such as the director's illness, cannot be helped, but the tardy entrance was avoidable, and the remote could have been tested before the presentation.

## ▶ RESTROOM FACILITIES AND RELATED CONSIDERATIONS

At the outset of the visit, show the guest which restrooms are nearest the presentation and autographing locations. Better yet, reserve a separate restroom for speakers—maybe a staff restroom or one in an office area off limits to students and the public. If there are multiple speakers, those not on stage might use the facilities before the general audience takes a break.

Consider restroom availability when planning the day's schedule. A 20-minute break may not be adequate. At one conference, the 350 participants solved their own problem. They agreed with the three men present that after the first ten minutes of the break, the men's room would become a ladies' room. They had already made a sign to post the change.

It's also a good idea to put extra rolls of towels and toilet tissue in the restroom so you don't need to look for the custodian when they run out.

## ▶ BOOK SALES

The most efficient way to handle book sales is to purchase them ahead of time (as suggested in "Obtaining Books for Autographing Sessions", pages 66-67). Advance sales put more books in the readers' hands during pre-visit activities, relieve uncertainty as to how many to order, and make book sales at the actual event less hectic.

If your event has advance registration, you can use offer the opportunity to order the books at a discount. Those who wait until the day of the event would pay the full retail price. Adult events often generate more sales on the day of the event. (See Form 12, Section 8, page 103, for a sample layout for sales and pick-up tables.) Schedule volunteers to work at the sales table throughout the day and post signs to clearly mark the traffic pattern. Include in the printed program an order form like the one sent out with the registration materials. The buyer hands the order to the salesperson, who fills the order, marks the slip "Paid," hands it to the buyer to keep as a receipt, and records the sale on a calculator or adding machine. The tape will reflect gross receipts when you take the end-of-the-conference inventory.

At large conferences or festivals, most book sales will take place at the beginning of the event and during breaks, lunch, and other times when speakers are not presenting. Plan to have enough salespeople to handle the volume of sales you anticipate, and have the following materials on hand:

- Calculator or adding machine with a paper tape for each cashier station. (Two or three may be necessary.)
- "Paid" stamps for each cashier.
- Money box for each cashier station. On the inside lid of each box, tape a note indicating the amount of cash provided as change. (At the end of the conference take that amount of cash out of the box before reconciling the register tape with the cash in the box.)
- Pencils for buyers to fill out book orders and for cashiers to check off items as the order is filled.
- Red pens for the person who checks each order before the buyer hands it to the cashier. The "checker" can also total the order, simplifying the procedure for the cashier.

Try to recruit volunteers who can step in and assist at either the book sales or autographing sessions so the event runs smoothly.

## ▶ AUTOGRAPHING SESSIONS

Autographing sessions go more smoothly if the author/illustrator does not have to open the books to the title page, move the books from one side to the other, manage the lines of people requesting autographs, or decipher verbal requests for a dedication message. Have the host serve as autograph assistant or designate others, perhaps students, for this duty, and be sure they understand their role. If students are helping, an adult should be nearby to handle decisions, if necessary.

Often an author/illustrator will bring a favorite autographing pen, but be sure to have some available. Some artists favor fine-line felt-tipped pens, but since they sometimes bleed through the page, most prefer a good quality ballpoint pen. Have a choice from which the guest can choose.

### JAN BRETT
**The Mitten**
**The Wild Christmas Reindeer**
**Annie and the Wild Animals**
**Berlioz the Bear**

"At one book signing three teachers asked me to consider doing a version of *The Mitten*."
— Jan Brett (1992)

Brett considered their suggestion and did illustrate a version of the folktale, *The Mitten* (Putnam, 1989). The story had two elements that Brett liked, snow and animals. Her version of the Ukrainian tale features a mole, rabbit, hedgehog, owl, badger, fox, and bear who squeeze into a little boy's mitten. The mouse is the last animal to arrive, and when he sits on the bear's nose, the bear sneezes and all the animals and the mitten go flying into the air. Jan Brett is a favorite conference speaker and often sketches as she talks about her art work. In addition to the usual background information, Brett's Web site at <http://www.jan-brett.com> includes interactive activities. Visitors can also subscribe to her newsletter.

Collectors value books autographed on the title page. Sometimes authors/illustrators have a preference as to where they autograph the books. In the absence of any specific request, open them to the title page for autographing.

In school visits, handle staff requests for autographs during a special welcoming reception or staff autographing session. The day's schedule needs to include time for the author to autograph the books sold both that day and through pre-sales. Some will want to continue to allow students to come to a central location to get their books autographed. However, others don't want to meet with students who have money to purchase books and not with others who don't have money. The solution? Autograph request slips. With these, the guest can autograph the books, and they can be returned to classrooms for distribution. If you use autograph request slips, you'll need to collect the books and leave them for autographing at a time when students are not present. In scheduling time for autographing, be sure to consider the number of books to be autographed and the limits of the visitor's time. It is often best not to schedule all the autographing for one extended session; the author's/illustrator's hand might get tired!

Have students fill out autographing slips even if you do have them come to the library or other site to have their books autographed. Anyone who has ever asked primary-aged children (or older students or adults, for that matter) their names will understand. How would a person know how to spell Deborah (or is it Debra?); Suzanne or Susanne; Leigh or Lea; Shawn, Shaun, or Sean? With all the variations in spelling and pronunciation, there are bound to be many misspelled dedications. Autograph slips reduce the times authors/illustrators have to ask, "How do you spell that?" See Forms 14 and 15 in Section 8, page 105-106 for sample autograph slips.

Requests for autographs on pieces of paper, in notebooks, are usually not appropriate. Discuss this point with students prior to the visit. However, if someone makes this type of request, the hostess will need to remind him that the author will autograph only books. Don't let the author/illustrator be put in the position of having to refuse this type of request. However, the child's desire for a personal connection is a sincere one that can be acknowledged with a friendly comment, a pat on the shoulder, or other gesture. Some authors/illustrators are very good about recognizing and responding to those needs. However, once he autographs a notebook or piece of paper, he will be swamped with requests, and it will be almost impossible to cut off the flow. Having a card or illustration for the child to take home as a memento is often the answer.

Sometimes autographing problems occur at adult functions. Someone will show up with a book or many books she did not purchase at the conference and expect them to be autographed. A committee operating a well-planned conference will have ordered a specific number of books based on the amount of time the author/illustrator has to autograph the books purchased at the conference. Since books brought in from outside do not benefit the conference, but *may* motivate reading, it is a difficult problem.

After struggling with the best way to handle this question, one of our planning committees came to a workable compromise. We allow the person to leave the books with dedication information written on a *plain piece of paper*. We do not supply autographing slips as the plain paper helps to identify the "outside" books. Those books are then put at the end of the line and do not move ahead of any books purchased at the conference. They will not be autographed until all of those purchased at the conference have been autographed. The person leaving the books must understand that they may or may not be autographed. This policy avoids direct confrontation but does not penalize anyone who purchases books at the conference.

Slips of paper presented by adults who expect autographs is another matter. As a matter of principle, I don't think adults should be treated any differently than younger participants who make the same type of request. Because fewer adults are present, this is not much of a concern at school visits. But at adults events, there are bound to be some incidents where you'll need to make a decision. It is wise to have discussed the possibilities with the planning committee and to have decided on a course of action before the problem occurs on the day of the event. Many authors, such as Rosemary Wells, do not want to sign paperbacks, let alone pieces of paper. It is part of the hostess's job to see that the guest is not put in the position of having to refuse such a request.

However, early on I vividly remember being at a conference where a well-known Caldecott Award-winner was speaking. In an effort to sell his books, he indicated that he was available after his presentation to sign books; in fact, he said, "I'll sign anything put in front of me." One young college student did not have the money to purchase his book but took the speaker at his word and asked him to sign a copy of the poster his publisher had sent. The illustrator not only refused to sign the poster but put down the student for even thinking that someone of his importance would have time to sign posters. The host, showing a lot more understanding than the guest, said, "I realize he indicated he would sign anything, but perhaps he did not realize that everyone would have a poster to be signed. I'm sorry for the misunderstanding."

The lesson(s)? Not all authors/illustrators are easy to deal with and not all problems are created by the participants.

At larger author/illustrator events where most of the books sold have not been pre-ordered, you may need to have bookplates available. Generally it is not financially prudent to begin to take orders for specific titles of books when there are still titles by the author/illustrator available for purchase and autographing. But if they are sold out and the author/illustrator still has time to autograph additional books, she might autograph book plates to be placed in books ordered during the conference. If you take book orders, collect the payment so that when the books arrive, you can attach the book plates before you send or deliver the books to those who ordered them.

Autographing at workshops and other large events is best handled without having individuals stand in line. The author/illustrator can autograph much more efficiently if not expected to socialize at the same time. Purchasers select the titles they wish to have autographed and then fill out an autograph form, which is placed inside the appropriate book and left at a designated location. (Hang a sign that says, "Leave Books Here for Autographing.") Volunteers then move the books to the guest artist, being careful to keep them in the order in which they were received. (The first books left for autographing should be the first autographed.)

At the autographing table, an assistant opens the book to the title page and places the autograph slip to the left of the title page. The author/illustrator signs a book and slides it to the right, where a volunteer places it on a book cart, alphabetically by first letter of the purchaser's last name. Another volunteer slides another open book from the left. This process goes on as long as necessary.

**STEVEN KELLOGG**
*Island of the Skog*
*A Penguin Pup for Pinkerton*
*The Missing Mitten Mystery*

At one conference, Steven Kellogg's plane was delayed and because of the weather, his return flight had to be moved up, so his time for autographing following his presentation was severely limited. His publisher agreed to pay the postage to ship his books (with autograph slips) to his home and back to those who put return addresses on their autograph slips. The autograph slips were the reason this procedure worked so well. Only one book became separated from its autograph slip, and it was returned to the conference director, who figured out from the inscription whose book it was.

Volunteers take the books alphabetized on the cart to the pick-up tables, where conference participants retrieve them. The pick-up tables should have signs designating portions of the alphabet so that people don't have to look through all the books to find theirs. If there's insufficient wall space to hang signs, consider posting them on yardsticks stuck in sand-filled coffee cans that have been covered to fit in with the theme of the conference. Helium-filled balloons with letters of the alphabet stenciled on all sides work, too.

If more than one author/illustrator is speaking, some may need to autograph while another is speaking—when they'd rather be listening to the speaker. Accommodate this by setting up autographing tables at the back of the presentation area. The author/illustrator who is not speaking can continue to autograph while still hearing the presentation. You may need to provide table lamps for the autograph tables if the house lights are

> **LOREEN LEEDY**
> *Subtraction Action*
> *The Edible Pyramid*
> *Mapping Penny's World*
>
> During Loreen Leedy's visits to schools, she generally shows slides of her studio and the book in progress. Afterwards, she draws characters on the overhead and finally takes student requests to draw a new character. This drawing can be photocopied and given to each child as a souvenir of the day.

dimmed. You'll need three chairs at each table: one each for the person who will open the books, the author/illustrator, and the person who will take the books and organize them on the book cart for return to the pick-up tables.

## ▶ PROVIDING A KEEPSAKE FOR ALL CHILDREN

Especially in school visits, knowing that many students who can't afford a book would still like an autograph, you might ask the author/illustrator to pen an autographed message on a piece of school stationery that you can duplicate, with her permission. Make this request before the day of the visit and distribute the messages to classes on the day of the visit. A variation: Students could make bookmarks on which to duplicate the author's/illustrator's signature.

## ▶ EMERGENCY BOX

On the day of an author/illustrator visit, I am always grateful that I've prepared an emergency box of supplies. The day of the visit can get hectic. At the last minute, you might need a piece of paper to write a note or a magic marker to make a sign; the guest author may request a piece of tape to attach a note to a book. A small shoebox or large cloth book bag holds everything that I think might possibly be needed. The following are the items I generally put in the box:

- Sharpened pencils
- Scissors
- Ink pen
- Wide felt-tipped markers (red and black)
- Masking tape
- Transparent tape
- Liquid paper
- Fine point felt-tipped markers (black)
- Ink eraser
- Sticky notes
- Several sheets of letter-sized blank paper

If the author/illustrator plans on using overhead transparencies, be sure to include

- A set of colored water-soluble transparency markers,
- A set of colored permanent transparency markers (to use if one of the speakers makes a sketch on a transparency), and
- A few sheets of blank transparency film.

Even if the event is being held in your own school, the emergency box will give you one place to find most needed items. At a site away from your home base, the emergency box is even more important.

Those in charge of selling books will need their own box of supplies, including

- Calculators for each person who will be checking orders and making sales,
- Pencils and pens,
- Cash boxes,
- Start-up cash,
- Paper for figuring, and
- Receipt book.

## ▶ THE BIG DAY

You've planned meticulously. There's not much left to do when the day finally arrives. The results of your planning are already visible. Welcome banners hang in the foyer. Students' stories and drawings—their responses to the author's/illustrator's books—line the halls. You've got an exciting day in store. Enjoy!

# After the Visit

## ▶ THINGS TO DO

Make sure honorarium payments and expense reimbursements to the author/illustrator are made promptly. Unless other arrangements are made, you should pay the author's honorarium at the conclusion of the visit. If you send the author/illustrator a statement of the agreed-upon honorarium (See Form 5, Section 8, page 95) in advance of the visit, he can sign and return it and the check can be ready. Initiate the paperwork to reimburse expenses as soon as possible after he leaves.

Though it's not required, sending the author/illustrator your personal letter of thanks and including a picture or two of the day's events is a gesture that almost everyone appreciates. Encourage students to write thank-you notes as well.

If the guest is an illustrator and has left behind a sketch or drawing for the school, make arrangements to have it matted and framed. For a nominal fee, you can have a metal plate inscribed the with the artist's name and date of the visit and attached to the frame.

Gather press clippings; photos; written comments from children, parents, and adult participants; and publicity flyers—anything having to do with the visit—and put them in a scrapbook. Display some of the photos and mementos on a bulletin board reflecting on the author/illustrator day and the activities that preceded it. Students might help create this display, incorporating their responses. Enlarge a favorite picture of the author/illustrator during the visit to frame and put in an "author's gallery" as a lasting memento of the day.

Include some of these materials on your school's Internet site. Harrison Elementary School in Cedar Rapids, Iowa has done just that for each author or illustrator who has visited the school. Check its site at <http://www.cr.k12.ia.us/harr/author.html>. Each author's page is a scrapbook of the author and the day's success. Some authors showcase school visits on their Web sites. Check Craig Brown's Web site at <http://www. geocities.com/ craigbrown_2000/

vanburen.html> for his visit to Van Buren Elementary. If any children are recognizable in the photographs, as they are on Brown's page at <http://www.geocities.com/craigbrown_2000/harrison.html>, be sure that you have signed permission slips for putting their pictures on the Web. (And be sure the permission slip has your school's attorney's approval.) Have a form available for the author/illustrator to sign, as well, giving you permission to post his photos on your Web site.

Once your scrapbook and Web pages are completed, look back on a job well done.

## ▶ EVALUATION: HOW DID THE VISIT GO?

The evaluation of an author visit is intended to look forward as well as back. Assess the process of planning and organizing this author/illustrator event. How did everything go? You will probably be able to evaluate the efficiency and effectiveness of the organization. Reactions to the presentation and the quality of the presentation will be evident, also.

But evaluating the day itself is just one part of the overall assessment. Review the goals the planning committee identified under "why?" during initial planning. Are you and your colleagues any closer to reaching those goals than when you began preparing for the event? What occurred? What do you think students have gained? Make a list of your and your colleagues' observations.

In the case of workshops and conferences, I am not inclined to ask participants to fill out a written evaluation. I have found that oral comments usually indicate the general feel for the day. Written evaluations, regardless of how well worded, simply give participants an opportunity to tell planners that the room was too cold (an equal number will say it was too warm), the lunch was not to their liking (others will like it), or they should have had an extra bulb on hand when the projector bulb blew. But that is simply my view; others will feel that a written evaluation gives valuable information. As a frequent speaker myself, I don't think you can expect the speaker to want the feedback. If she was successful, she will know it from the audience's body language, smiles, and applause. If he was not, he'll already be painfully aware of it. At that point, there is little he can do to change anything. So give speakers the luxury of feeling good about themselves and the day.

In any case, write down accomplishments and anecdotes that you can share when you need specifics for another author/illustrator event. Write these thoughts and evaluative comments as soon after the day as possible; the more time passes, the more difficult it will be to recall specific incidents.

## ▶ A FINAL WORD

Always remember to send a letter of thanks not only to the author/illustrator but also to the cosponsors of the events and to anyone at the publishing house with whom you worked.

Let the publicist know if the visit was a success; share positive anecdotes. Don't overlook thanking administrators for their support and encouragement. Be sure to give credit to each of the staff who helped make the event a meaningful one. Send a memo thanking everyone for a great job. Mention names and special projects—and try to find something positive to say about everyone's involvement.

### *To the Visiting Artist*

Arrange ahead of time for a few classrooms to write thank-you letters and include pictures and comments from the day. Collect these contributions and send them to the author in one large brown envelope with adequate postage. As for pictures or other memorabilia the children want the author/illustrator to have, send that to her home rather than expecting her to fit it into her luggage.

A nice gesture is to include photos of the author/illustrator during the visit, especially ones that might be appropriate for a "school visit brochure." Visiting authors cannot take photos of themselves during a visit and usually don't have someone along who can. If the photos include children, go the extra step and include parent permissions for the author to use the photos in publicity material. Or at least indicate that you will get the signatures if the author/illustrator wants them.

## To The Sponsors

Of course, you thank sponsors who give dollars or in-kind donations for a program when you receive the donation. However, I also suggest that you send a second thank-you note after the event. The benefactor will appreciate it if you enclose newspaper articles or people's comments in the note. Since you will have sent the requisite thank-you when you received the donation, he will view this second note as truly sincere, not perfunctory. Let him know how much he contributed to the program's success. By all means, include a copy of any announcement or printed program that acknowledges his gift. This follow-up thank-you is surely not too much for a corporation or an individual who has gone out of his way to support your program.

## To Others Who Contributed Time, Ideas, and Support

Don't overlook a brief note to everyone who helped make the day a success. Send a thank-you to the custodian who carried in the books and made sure the bathrooms didn't run out of toilet tissue. Thank the kitchen workers who prepared the lunch or developed a special menu in honor of the author/illustrator. Make sure each staff member who played a part in the visit is given a personal note of thanks for her contribution—the physical education teacher who did extra playground duty so another teacher could have his class settled in time for an author/illustrator session, or the teacher whose class knew the guest artist's books and asked well-thought-out questions. Thank volunteers for everything from making the cake for staff reception to taking photos throughout the day.

Letting people know that their contributions are valued will help them realize how much your own efforts contributed to the success of the day.

# No Excuses

After your success with a real live author visit, you may find yourself wanting to repeat the experience next year but being unable to afford it. Funding sources often don't want to fund the same type of activity two years in a row. Whatever the situation, don't let yourself find excuses for not repeating the success each year. The rewards in reading will make it worthwhile.

Sponsors might be willing to finance a program with a little different twist. They may want the visit to benefit a wider audience. Perhaps they would fund another author visit if a community presentation were part of the plans. Giving the event a technology connection might fit with an organization's goals for helping integrate technology into the schools. Inviting a writer with a career emphasis might attract some additional support. Maybe a local historical society would underwrite a conference featuring authors of books set within the state.

Whatever the twist, begin to think about what event you could plan. Perhaps it will be a Young Readers' Conference (a variation on the young authors' conference) or an authors' festival featuring local authors/illustrators. Perhaps you can arrange a video conference or a telephone call using a speaker phone. Arrange the latter in much the same way you would schedule an in-person visit; that is, contact the publicist or author/illustrator and schedule a time that you and your class may call. E-mail interviews might be another possibility. Some authors/illustrators ask for a small honorarium for their time, while others will give interviews gratis. Be sure to ask; don't assume anything.

To get a feel for the excitement generated by author visits, talk to others who have hosted them. Checking with colleagues is most useful, but many experiences are posted on the World Wide Web as well. Check out the Web site "Authors Visit Schools." The New York City schools hosted several authors during 1998 and posted responses at <http://www.newvisions.org/astrau.html>.

Some of the visits were online; other authors/illustrators visited in person—just two of the ways you can bring an author into your classroom or library.

## ▶ VISITS USING COMMUNICATIONS NETWORKS

One Iowa school arranged to visit with Janet Stevens in Colorado over an interactive communications network. The class traveled to a local area education agency where a communications network was available. The room had 25 microphones and other video and audio components. Janet Stevens spoke from a studio in her hometown. The class asked her questions and she showed them some of her new artwork. The cost was nominal as it did not involve more than a couple of hours of the author's time, and there was no travel expense. The class had to fund bus transportation to the network site and pay a nominal fee to use the system.

This electronic visit was the culmination of a very successful author focus unit. Your community may have similar networks. Inviting an author to participate in such a visit will take some coordination at the author's location, and you may need to establish a liaison there. The author's publicist may be able to assist with the initial contacts and put you in touch with helpful people in the author's area.

## ▶ ONLINE VISITS

Scholastic Network regularly offers online visits with featured authors or illustrators. Some of the visits are live chats with the author actually present in a chat room at a specific time and day. Students can log on, ask the author/illustrator questions, and get answers in real time. This works very well with a large screen. Questions and Answers are shown online. Since many logins are possible, several classrooms can participate if they have an Internet connection. Some situations require other arrangements—classrooms that share an Internet connection or selected small groups or individuals from a number of classrooms.

With one connection or several, it is important to prepare for the visit no less than you would with a full classroom of learners. In our school, three classrooms of second and third graders wanted to participate in an online chat with Joanna Cole, author of the *Magic School Bus* series, but the school had only one connection. Each classroom read about Cole and read the *Magic School Bus* books, along with some of her other titles. As a class, they made a list of questions they wanted to ask the author.

On the day of the online visit, two representatives from each class came to the library media center, where the connection was available, with clipboards and sheets of each class's questions. The library media specialist logged the group into the chat and helped them type in their questions and keep track of what questions had been asked. If one group asked a question that was on another's list, the child with the clipboard simply checked it off so we did not ask it again. They did not have to keep track of the answers because we captured the chat and printed it afterward. Eventually all the questions on all the lists were asked and answered.

When the chat was over, the children returned to their classrooms while the library media specialist formatted the text of the chat so it was easy to read and then printed two to three copies for each classroom. The classroom teachers used the copies to discuss the questions and answers with their entire classes. It was an exciting activity because each child had the satisfaction of having his question answered.

To find out about current online visits scheduled by Scholastic, go to its site at <http://www.scholastic.com>. That same site, at times, offers the opportunity for anyone to post a question for a specific author. The questions are forwarded to the author, who answers 20 to 30 of them and returns them to the publisher. Scholastic posts them as an interview.

This is an adaptation of the bulletin-board type of interview in which students can post their questions on a common board visible to all visitors. At intervals throughout a designated time (two weeks or so), the featured author reads the questions on the bulletin board and responds to them, posting them back to the board for all to view. Another organization, the Read In Foundation, hosts author chats during the school year and a tremendous reading day, "The Read In," in the spring of each year. Connect with these fabulous author activities at <http://www.readin.org>.

As with all interactions with authors and illustrators, students must be prepared to ask questions based on information they have taken the time to learn. During one bulletin board discussion with Katherine Paterson, students asked questions such as "How many books have you written?" "Do you write picture books or chapter books?" and other questions that showed they were not prepared to interact with the author in a meaningful way. One of Paterson's comments suggested that a reference session at the library might be appropriate.

Her comment affirmed what most educators believe: the opportunity to ask questions should not substitute for research but should expand on what students have learned from reading reference works and books by the author. An opportunity to ask questions can cap an author focus just as an in-person author visit does and should reflect similar preparation.

## ▷ U.S. MAIL OR E-MAIL

Encourage students who become interested in specific authors/illustrators to write letters to them, via either e-mail or U.S. mail. You can often find e-mail addresses on the author's/illustrator's Web site, which sometimes provides a U.S. mail address as well. Jim Aylesworth's site at <http://www.ayles.com> gives both his e-mail and mailing address as well as his phone number. Betsy Byars's site at <http://www.betsybyars.com> states that she does not have an e-mail address but she does provide a U.S. mailing address. Others may post an address for writing them in care of their publisher.

An entire class might write a "class letter" collaboratively on the overhead, revise it, edit it, and have one student copy it for all to sign. Please do not ask each child to copy the letter and certainly do not send 26 copies of virtually the same letter to the author/illustrator. If individual students want to write their own letters to the same author, mail them, unfolded, in a single envelope, and supply a self-addressed stamped envelope in case the author/illustrator wants to reply.

Students who write an author/illustrator may need some guidance as to what to write about. Authors and illustrators always welcome statements about a reader's genuine interest in their work. They don't welcome requests for free materials or books. Make student correspondents aware that authors/illustrators have to pay for books, photos, or anything else they send. Requests for posters of the author's/illustrator's books or brochures about the author should go to the publisher. Not all authors/illustrators have time to answer letters. For those who do, the cost of postage adds up, so do include a self-addressed stamped envelope in case the author/illustrator does want to reply.

Don't let students assume that they'll get a reply to e-mail, either. Replying to e-mail is also time-consuming, and many authors receive literally hundreds of e-mails and letters a month. If they took the time to respond to all of them, they would not have time to write their books. If they print a student's e-mail to respond to it later, they must pay for paper, cartridge ink, and computer time. Just as with letters sent via U. S. mail, it is more convenient to send e-mail messages in one batch.

"Dear Author," an article by Marion Dane Bauer (*School Library Journal,* March 1993, p. 144), should be required reading for all teachers who encourage their students to write to an author/illustrator. Bauer addresses some of the same topics that Beverly Cleary covers in "Dear Author, Answer this letter now…" (*Instructor,* November/December 1985, pp. 22-25). Cleary dislikes letters with numerous questions she is expected to answer and, even more, the trend to require children to tell the author what they didn't like about a book and how it could be improved. She detests the pressure from writ-

> **DEBORAH HOPKINSON**
> *Sweet Clara and the Freedom Quilt*
> *Under the Quilt of Night*
> *Fannie in the Kitchen*
>
> "I love to respond to students' questions via e-mail. It can be a great way to generate interest in reading and writing."
> —Deborah Hopkinson
>
> Deborah Hopkinson can be reached through her Web site at <http://www.people.whitman.edu/~hopkinda/>. She makes in-person visits to schools and libraries as well.

ers who say, "I get extra credit if you answer in your own handwriting," or "If you don't answer, I get a bad grade."

Cleary describes a reading incentive program in which students are paid play money for reading. At the end of the year, they use the money to purchase items donated by authors/illustrators. After the idea was published in a national periodical, authors and illustrators were deluged with requests for personal mementos and belongings. Cleary describes letters that demand answers and others that chastise her for not answering their letters personally. (She often sent a publisher's brochure that answered questions most often asked).

Both Bauer and Cleary make valid points you should consider before encouraging young readers to send a letter off to an author/illustrator. There is nothing wrong with helping a child to understand that a particular question or comment is not appropriate. That is our job. If a young person wishes to write a letter or e-mail, help him write a letter the author/illustrator will enjoy and appreciate.

Deborah Hopkinson (<http://people.whitman.edu/~hopkinda/>) is an author of historical fiction who regularly offers e-mail connections as an alternative to in-person visits.

## ▶ BOOKSTORE VISITS

Bookstores bring in authors and illustrators for book signings that are open to the public and groups of school children. On the downside, these visits are often publicized only a few days in advance and often take place on weekends or in the evenings. On the other hand, many parents, if asked, are willing to get their children to a book signing. Call local outlets of major chains as well as independent booksellers to find out if they have a schedule of author/illustrator visits and if they'll put you on their mailing lists for newsletters or announcements. Watch the newspaper; check for announcements when you're in the store.

Once you become aware of an author visit to a bookstore, plan to incorporate it into classroom or community activities. Bookstores sometimes will cooperate with schools, museums, or art centers to bring in an author to enhance a specific program or exhibit.

If you can arrange for students to visit with the author/illustrator at the bookstore, your preparation will be much the same as if the author/illustrator were coming to your school, except that the children involved might be a single class or a group selected on another criterion, such as an interest in art. Once you determine the group, plan reading and other activities relating to the author/illustrator and culminating in the visit. After the book signing, write thank-you letters to the store, the author/illustrator, and the parents who got the students to the function.

Some Web sites will tell you if an author/illustrator is to be in your area. HarperCollins offers a search page at <http://www.harperchildrens.com/hch/author/> where visitors can look for authors coming to their areas. The lists are often minimal but periodically will have information that can help connect you to an author event. Every lead is worth checking. Individual author sites also offer information. For example, Jane Kurtz has an appearance page at <http://www.janekurtz.com> that is usually up-to-date and tells where she is going to appear. Knowing an author is coming to your area, you may be able to arrange a corollary event.

# ▶ MUSEUMS AND ART CENTERS

In several instances, schools in our area have capitalized on exhibits at our local art museum. The first was of original art from the Babar series. Subsequent exhibits featured the work of Dr. Seuss (Theodor Seuss Geisel), Eric Carle's collages, Navajo artist Shonto Begay, Czech native Peter Sis, and the Pinkney family—Jerry, Gloria, Brian, and Andrea Davis Pinkney. Our city is relatively small (population 110,000), but it has a very active museum staff that has been responsible for originating some of these exhibits and bringing in other traveling exhibits. In conjunction with most of the exhibits, the staff has arranged for teacher workshops and has encouraged school groups to schedule tours.

Being able to preview an exhibit and schedule class tours allows us to integrate material about the author/illustrator and his work into classroom and library activities. For example, with Begay's exhibit we focused on the Southwest, studying its geography, learning about its history, and reading other stories set in the area. Younger children read Gerald McDermott's Pueblo tale *Arrow to the Sun* (Viking, 1974) and older students read Gloria Skurzynski's *Lost in Devil's Desert*. (Beech Tree, 1993). All read and shared Begay's picture books set in the same area. We read Begay's poems in *Navajo: visions and voices across the Mesa* (Scholastic, 1995) and enjoyed the wonderful watercolors in that book as well as in others, such as Caron Lee Cohen's *The Mud Pony: A Traditional Skidi Pawnee Tale* (Scholastic, 1988).

One classroom teacher toured the exhibit, attended the teacher workshop, and shared information with her students. In the workshop Begay had pointed out how colors in the books varied from the original art and told how he came to develop some of the images. When the class visited the exhibit, they were well prepared to see for themselves. Their joy at discovering some of the elements they had discussed in class was infectious. They noted the Southwestern artists' color choices and discussed the moods they conveyed. They could see texture and other subtle differences between original art and photographic reproductions in books. They asked intelligent questions and discussed the answers with their teacher, who had immersed herself in learning about the exhibit.

We had similar experiences with the Eric Carle, Pinkney, and other exhibits. They enabled young readers to tie pictures with text and use both to express themselves.

In a sense this museum visit was an author visit, and in a sense it was not. The children did not get to meet the artist but did learn about him vicariously through their teacher. In many ways the experience was even more beneficial than a face-to-face visit because the class could progress at their own pace and complete the unit on their own time. They could schedule activities to suit themselves.

In fact, one class scheduled a trip to the Begay exhibit as an introductory activity. They toured the exhibit, viewed the paintings, and took notes. Back in the classroom, they read about the author and his work. In his books, they found the images that they had seen in the exhibit. When

### NICOLE RUBEL
*Rotten Ralph*
*Cyrano the Bear*
*A Cowboy Named Ernestine*

Nicole Rubel is one of those versatile artists/illustrators who can successfully address audiences of all ages. Her Web site at <http://www.nicolerubel.com> describes the topics on which she is prepared to speak. One of her presentations targeted at a younger audience is titled "The Rotten Ralph Program." The *Rotten Ralph* books are the focus. The program ends with a question-and-answer session and a "Goodbye, Rotten Ralph" dance. If Rubel is asked to speak to high school readers and adults, she often talks about "the metamorphosis." After introducing her audience to her books, home, and studio, she illustrates with slides her metamorphosis from a nonspeaking twin to an artist, writer, and speaker and tells how a classroom assignment by an excellent teacher changed her life.

they returned for another visit to the exhibit, they took along books and compared the original art to the printed pages, finding elements in the book art similar to paintings that Begay did as fine art pieces. Their return trip to the exhibit made it doubly effective.

Older students can also learn from exhibits of and presentations by illustrators. Many of them have programs tailored to intermediate, secondary, and adult audiences.

While an author visit of some sort is the perfect way to finish an author focus, such a culmination is not absolutely necessary. There are many other options, ranging from simple "reading fests" to museum exhibits to video conferencing. Plan a monthly focus on a favorite or soon-to-be favorite author/illustrator and celebrate at the conclusion of the focus. Conclude a focus on an author or illustrator who is no longer living with a read-in, a video or film of one of her books, or a special luncheon. Paul Galdone, Dr. Seuss, Beatrix Potter, Barbara Cooney, or Verna Aardema could be the subject of such a focus. Finish the unit by reading Paul Galdone's nursery folktales and have a character day when each child comes dressed as a character from one of his books. Read Dr. Seuss and serve green eggs and ham for breakfast. After reading Beatrix Potter's books, enjoy fresh bread and blackberry jam with a little chamomile tea and reread the class's favorite tale. Other author/illustrator focuses can culminate with simple celebrations involving reading, cookies, and milk.

Celebrate favorite authors and illustrators and learn about new ones. Read, investigate, enjoy. The fun and learning have just begun.

# Forms

On the following pages are forms you may duplicate or adapt for planning and keeping track of arrangements for your own author's/illustrator's visit. Not every committee will want to use all of the forms, but they may help to remind you of in-house forms or procedures required by your organization.

## FORM 1 — BENEFITS OF AN AUTHOR/ILLUSTRATOR FOCUS

- Motivates reading and writing and other responses to literature.
- Gives young readers a positive experience with reading and writing.
- Builds enthusiasm for an in-depth experience with literary selections.
- Puts reading and writing in the spotlight—on an equal basis with sports and music.
- Provides opportunities for a real audience to respond to reading.
- Produces opportunities for developing planning skills and cooperative learning.
- Offers a structure for sharing literature through reading and other activities that fulfill curriculum or program goals.
- Develops a respect for the body of a writer's or illustrator's work.
- Reveals connections among the author's/illustrator's works.
- Makes the entire library a potential reading source as children search for more of the author's work and for other books with connecting themes.
- Creates a sense of achievement as readers begin to recognize connections in the works of different writers and identify universal themes and topics.
- Challenges minds to think in new terms as each connection is found.
- Brings more books and reading into the curriculum.

**FORM 2** **AUTHOR/ILLUSTRATOR VISIT: CHECKLIST AND TIME LINE**

## PLANNING (SIX MONTHS TO A YEAR IN ADVANCE)

\_\_\_\_\_ Gather information and fill in Author/Illustrator Appearance Worksheet.
\_\_\_\_\_ Make initial contact with publicist, marketing director, or author/illustrator.
\_\_\_\_\_ Finalize the schedule of days the author/illustrator will be in your community, negotiate the honorarium, agree upon expectations for the visit, and follow up with a written agreement.
\_\_\_\_\_ Reserve facilities. Get all agreements in writing.
\_\_\_\_\_ Request available promotional material from the publisher.
\_\_\_\_\_ Develop promotional material and focus materials for the visit. Discuss with coordinating committee and decide who will be responsible for

    \_\_\_\_\_ Travel and lodging
    \_\_\_\_\_ Local transportation
    \_\_\_\_\_ Meal functions associated with events
    \_\_\_\_\_ Personal escorts for the visiting artist
    \_\_\_\_\_ Ordering books (liaison with book dealer or publishing house)
    \_\_\_\_\_ Developing and distributing in-house resource materials
    \_\_\_\_\_ Schedule coordination
    \_\_\_\_\_ Publicity and public relations
    \_\_\_\_\_ Record of events (historian), including arrangements for a photographer

## PREPARATION (TWO TO THREE MONTHS IN ADVANCE)

\_\_\_\_\_ Begin in-house promotion. Schools begin the focus unit.
\_\_\_\_\_ Order books directly from publisher or through local book dealer.
\_\_\_\_\_ Make plane and hotel reservations, first asking the author's/illustrator's preferences.
\_\_\_\_\_ Send tentative itinerary to author/illustrator and publisher for approval. Send copies of confirmation to author/illustrator and publisher (no less than one month in advance).
- Include plane tickets and hotel confirmation numbers along with the address and phone numbers of the hotel.
- Send expense form to author/illustrator, asking her to attach receipts for all expenses except the honorarium. Fill in the honorarium amount.
- Send name of the person who will meet the author/illustrator at the airport. Include both business and home phone numbers and other local contacts in case of emergency.

\_\_\_\_\_ Make reservations or arrangements for all meal functions.
\_\_\_\_\_ Finalize plans for all other aspects of the visit. (See list of committee members' responsibilities.)
\_\_\_\_\_ Check with custodians of all facilities concerning room set-up, equipment needs, and seating requirements. Verify availability of needed number of chairs, suitable type of microphones, and other equipment. Decide who will be responsible for reserving equipment.

## LAST DETAILS (TWO TO THREE WEEKS BEFORE THE DAY)

\_\_\_\_\_ Contact the author/illustrator or publisher to make sure he has received all travel confirmations. Check for any changes in plans, such as equipment needs.
\_\_\_\_\_ Check that the books for autographing have arrived.
\_\_\_\_\_ Verify that autographing forms have been printed and are ready for the autographing sessions.
\_\_\_\_\_ Reconfirm arrangements for facilities where events will be held.
\_\_\_\_\_ Be sure that the author's/illustrator's honorarium will be available on the day of the visit or make arrangements with the author/illustrator for an alternative payment date.
\_\_\_\_\_ Make sure the person picking up the author/illustrator has a copy of the flight schedule.
\_\_\_\_\_ Create a folder for yourself that contains:
- An extra blank copy of expense form.
- List of contacts with telephone numbers for the author/illustrator, publicists, local hosts, escorts.
- Address of hotel or motel where reservations have been made.
- Copy of itinerary for the author/illustrator visit.

- Copy of the author's/illustrator's flight schedule (arrival and departure).
- Copy of any catering arrangements with contact name and phone number.

_____ Confirm any arrangements that have been made for meals.
_____ Check that all equipment, signs, facilities have been reserved or arranged for.
_____ Order corsages or flowers and arrange for someone to pick them up.
_____ Encourage classes to display author/illustrator-related projects and welcoming banners in hallways.

### ONE DAY BEFORE THE AUTHOR'S/ILLUSTRATOR'S FIRST EVENT IN YOUR COMMUNITY

_____ Put the folder containing your copies of all contracts and contact phone numbers in your attaché case.
_____ Pick up the honorarium check and deposit it in a safe place where you can retrieve it in a timely fashion at the end of the visit.
_____ Check the final set-up for sessions tomorrow, including audiovisual equipment, seating arrangements, microphone, and podium.
_____ Verify author/illustrator local transportation arrangements.
_____ Verify availability of the author's/illustrator's escort and review duties with that person.
_____ Remind photographer and verify that ample film will be available.
_____ Check that welcoming banner is in place and, if you are planning a morning reception, that someone plans to start the coffee in time.
_____ Review all plans for tomorrow's events. No detail is too small to double-check.
_____ Verify all arrangements with the custodians in regard to all set-up and facility needs. Make sure assistance will be available for carrying materials the author/illustrator plans to bring. (You may want to arrange for a cart.)

### THE DAY

_____ Enjoy!

### AFTER THE AUTHOR/ILLUSTRATOR LEAVES:

_____ Write and send personal letters of thanks to
- The author/illustrator
- The publicist at the publishing house
- All committee members
- Administrators who supported the visit
- Sponsors
- All staff members who helped in any way
- Custodians and other support staff who assisted
- Volunteers
- Secretaries who responded to queries, answered the phone, typed correspondence

_____ Offer to mail student written thank-yous to sponsors and to the author/illustrator.
_____ Take film for processing. Arrange a display of photographs of the day. Offer staff and participants the opportunity to purchase prints.
_____ Compile an archival file of materials and contracts relating to the event.
_____ Compile a scrapbook and bulletin board that will be accessible to others to look at. These might include brochures, photographs, and newspaper articles.
_____ Arrange to return any unsold books (immediately) and to settle accounts with the book dealer or publisher (whoever arranged to supply the books for the events).
_____ Request payment for all outstanding expenses, including reimbursement of expenses owed to the author/illustrator.
_____ Choose a photograph of the author/illustrator to enlarge and frame for your library, school, or office area.
_____ Make a list of things you would do differently next time. (Hopefully, the list is short.)
_____ Send a final memo to the staff/administrator sharing successes and anecdotes of the day and congratulating everyone for a job well done.

## FORM 3 — BUDGET WORKSHEET

**ESTIMATED**

Airfare from _____ to _____  $ _____

Motel/hotel _____ nights @ $ _____  $ _____

Ground transportation _____ $ _____

Meals _____ days @ $ _____  $ _____

Miscellaneous (telephone calls, postage)  $ _____

Total estimated expenses  $ _____

Maximum total honorarium that may be offered
_____ days @ $ _____  $ _____

Total budget for proposed visit  $ _____


## SOURCES OF FUNDING

### FUNDING SOURCE AND AMOUNT      MAXIMUM AVAILABLE

Source: _____  $ _____

Source: _____  $ _____

Source: _____  $ _____

Source: _____  $ _____

Source: _____  $ _____

Source: _____  $ _____

Source: _____  $ _____

Total amount from all funding sources  $ _____

## FORM 4 — ACCOUNTING LOG

page ____ of ____

| DATE | VENDOR/SOURCE AND PURPOSE | AMOUNT | BALANCE |
|------|---------------------------|--------|---------|
|      | Balance forward           |        |         |
|      |                           |        |         |
|      |                           |        |         |
|      |                           |        |         |
|      |                           |        |         |
|      |                           |        |         |
|      |                           |        |         |
|      |                           |        |         |
|      |                           |        |         |
|      |                           |        |         |
|      |                           |        |         |
|      |                           |        |         |
|      |                           |        |         |
|      |                           |        |         |
|      |                           |        |         |
|      |                           |        |         |
|      |                           |        |         |
|      |                           |        |         |
|      |                           |        |         |
|      |                           |        |         |
|      |             Balance to carry forward |  |     |

## FORM 5 — STATEMENT: EXPENSES AND HONORARIA

Date: ____/____/____

Name of organization: _____

Address: _____

_____

Phone number: _____

Purpose: _____
        ("Author/Illustrator Day" or title of event)

Authorized by: _____
              (Appropriate staff member)

Pay to: _____    _____
       (Name of author/illustrator)            (Social Security number)

Address: _____

_____

| DATE | ITEM | TRANS. | MEALS | | | MISC. | TOTAL |
|      |      |        | B | L | D |       |       |
|---|---|---|---|---|---|---|---|
|   |   |   |   |   |   |   |   |
|   |   |   |   |   |   |   |   |
|   |   |   |   |   |   |   |   |
|   |   |   |   |   |   |   |   |

Certified Correct: _____     Date billed: _____
                  (Signature of author/illustrator)

Approved: _____              Date paid: _____
         (Authorizing staff member)

Account Number: _____

## FORM 6 — WORKSHEET: SEARCH FOR POSSIBLE GRANTS OR COSPONSORS

_____ Schools in the same or adjoining districts

_____ Libraries in your community or in adjoining communities

_____ Library friends organizations

_____ Parent-teacher organizations

_____ Bookstores (Independent, locally owned stores are often more receptive.)

_____ Local businesses known for their community involvement

_____ Area education agencies or county or parish school systems

_____ Community art museums (particularly in the case of an illustrator visit)

_____ Private grant organizations

_____ Educational organizations (local chapters of the International Reading Association, Society of Children's Book Writers and Illustrators, or regional library organizations)

_____ Colleges

_____ State arts council

_____

_____

_____

_____

_____

## FORM 7 · WORKSHEET: TENTATIVE DATES FOR THE AUTHOR/ILLUSTRATOR VISIT

(Use a separate form for each set of suggested dates.)

Check one: _____ preferred dates _____ 1st alternative _____ 2nd alternative

Day 1 - Arrival            (M T W Th F)            Date _____

Day 2                      (M T W Th F)            Date _____

Day 3                      (M T W Th F)            Date _____

Day 4                      (M T W Th F)            Date _____

### CONTACTS TO CHECK FOR CONFLICTS

Organization _____ ph # (____) _____

Contact person: _____ Conflicts _____ no _____ yes

Organization _____ ph # (____) _____

Contact person: _____ Conflicts _____ no _____ yes

Organization _____ ph # (____) _____

Contact person: _____ Conflicts _____ no _____ yes

Organization _____ ph # (____) _____

Contact person: _____ Conflicts _____ no _____ yes

Organization _____ ph # (____) _____

Contact person: _____ Conflicts _____ no _____ yes

Organization _____ ph # (____) _____

Contact person: _____ Conflicts _____ no _____ yes

Organization _____ ph # (____) _____

Contact person: _____ Conflicts _____ no _____ yes

## FORM 8 — WORKSHEET: AUTHOR/ILLUSTRATOR APPEARANCE

Author(s): _____   Date of Inquiry: _____

Date(s) for Appearance: _____

    Alternative date(s): _____

Expectations for the Visit: Types of appearances, autograph sessions, number of days, etc.




Amount of Honorarium to be offered, per day: _____

Author(s): _____

Expenses that will be covered: _____

Audience (age, number, etc.): _____




Contact person: _____

School/Organization _____

Address: _____
_____

Phone: _____


Additional information:

## FORM 9  PHONE LOG

Log Page # _____

Date: _____ phone # (_____) _____

To whom: _____

RE: _____

Date: _____ phone # (_____) _____

To whom: _____

RE: _____

Date: _____ phone # (_____) _____

To whom: _____

RE: _____

Date: _____ phone # (_____) _____

To whom: _____

RE: _____

Date: _____ phone # (_____) _____

To whom: _____

RE: _____

Date: _____ phone # (_____) _____

To whom: _____

RE: _____

Date: _____ phone # (_____) _____

To whom: _____

RE: _____

Date: _____ phone # (_____) _____

## FORM 10  DIRECTORY INFORMATION INQUIRY LOG

1-area code-555-1212                                                      Inquiry Log page # _____

Date: _____        Area Code called (_____)

Name (publisher or author/illustrator): _____

Telephone no. _____        (address/city): _____

Notes _____

Date: _____        Area Code called (_____)

Name (publisher or author/illustrator): _____

Telephone no. _____        (address/city): _____

Notes _____

Date: _____        Area Code called (_____)

Name (publisher or author/illustrator): _____

Telephone no. _____        (address/city): _____

Notes _____

Date: _____        Area Code called (_____)

Name (publisher or author/illustrator): _____

Telephone no. _____        (address/city): _____

Notes _____

Date: _____        Area Code called (_____)

Name (publisher or author/illustrator): _____

Telephone no. _____        (address/city): _____

Notes _____

**FORM 11**

# Making the Most of an Author/Illustrator Visit

## *A Summary for Planning Committee Members*

### THE FIRST STEP

By the time you read this, you will have probably already taken the first step—making arrangements for the author/illustrator to visit your school. If you haven't already followed up with a letter confirming those arrangements, do so now. Be sure to include
- The date of the visit,
- Agreed-upon honorarium and expenses to be reimbursed,
- Who will make transportation arrangements—the author or the sponsoring organization,
- Expectations for the visit (type of audience; special requests, such as autographing sessions, staff welcoming reception, dinner with planning committee), and
- Site of the visit.

### ARRANGING FOR BOOKS

Part of the excitement of an author visit is being able to obtain an autographed book. Make arrangements at least three months before the author's visit to obtain books either directly from the publisher or through a local book distributor. The latter may be most efficient. A book dealer will know the procedures and will work with you to select the titles and estimate the number of books to order. Some book dealers offer a 20-25 percent discount.

### ARRANGEMENTS FOR RETURNING THE UNSOLD BOOKS

Sending home book order forms before the visit will help you estimate the number of books to order and will also help in building anticipation. Check with the book dealer or publisher to determine the final date books should be ordered. Arrange for booktalks in each classroom.

### FOCUSING ON THE AUTHOR/ILLUSTRATOR

Building a community of readers focusing on the author/illustrator's work is an important element in preparing for the author's visit. Involve as many staff members as possible in the planning stages. Plan activities to focus on the author's/illustrator's books and to keep the staff as involved as possible.

The first activity might be an introductory unit for use at each grade level. Depending on the author/illustrator, the introductory activity will most often include reading one of the books and some type of extension activity, such as an art experience, comparing this book to other books, writing a play, and reader's theater. Develop and share suggestions for using the other books so that children will be exposed to the broadest level of experiences possible.

Focusing on an author/illustrator helps to establish a structure for sharing literature in a manner consistent with curriculum or program goals. Students develop a respect for the body of work of a writer or illustrator. The entire library media center becomes a potential reading source as teachers and students begin to recognize the connections in the works of different writers and as they identify universal themes. When a connection is found between two books, the mind is challenged to think in new terms. The more the students and teachers learn about literature, the more ways they will fit literature into every subject area.

### WHAT QUESTIONS WILL YOU ASK?

Most authors/illustrators who visit schools welcome questions from students and teachers. During the last week or two before the author's/illustrator's visit, help students formulate questions. Younger students may need help in understanding the difference between questions and comments. Practice sessions will help students learn how to formulate appropriate questions. Points to review with students:
- Listen to questions as well as answers so you don't repeat a question.
- Ask questions based on information you know. For example, if the author does not also illustrate his books, you will not want to ask, "How long did it take you to draw the illustrations?"

## SCHEDULING THE DAY

Formulate a schedule a week or two before the author's/illustrator's visit. In general, four presentations of 40 to 60 minutes each are *maximum* for any one-day school visit. The sessions are simply too energy-consuming for a guest to do more than that. Authors/illustrators may request that only three sessions be scheduled.

Build in time to set up equipment that will be used during the presentation, breaks, lunch, and autographing sessions. Distribute the schedule to staff early enough to reconcile any problems before the day of the visit.

Notify appropriate news media well in advance. Supply background information about the author/illustrator, a schedule for the day, and the name of a contact person.

Plan to display student work related to the author/illustrator visit in rooms, hallways, and library. You may want to take pictures of the displays before the actual day.

## THE DAY OF THE VISIT

Often the author/illustrator will arrive the day before the school visit. Arrange for him to be met at the airport or point of arrival. It is hospitable to invite the guest for dinner, but don't be offended if he prefers to have time to work on projects he has brought along or to follow his own agenda.

Make arrangements for the guest to be met and transported to the school on the morning of the school visit. An escort should be available to be with the guest throughout the day. The duties of the escort include showing the author/illustrator to the appropriate locations throughout the building, introducing her at the beginnings of presentations, and concluding the sessions.

Details such as offering beverages throughout the day (Have water or another beverage available at all sessions), arranging for lunch, and facilitating the autographing sessions, are all part of the escort's duties. During any staff reception to welcome the guest, the escort would makes individual introductions and makes sure that the guest's time is not monopolized. In general, the escort's duties involve making the author/illustrator as comfortable as possible throughout the day and attending to details that will make the visit a memorable one for staff, students, and the author/illustrator.

If you want photos of the day's events, make those plans in advance. Consider asking a talented parent or student to be the official photographer. Videotape only with the author's/illustrator's permission.

## AUTOGRAPHING

The day's schedule should include time for the author/illustrator to autograph books. Staff requests for autographs should be handled in a separate staff reception or autograph session. Sometimes personal contact is not possible for all autograph requests. Autograph slips for dedication could be filled out for each book to be autographed.

Requests for autographs on pieces of paper are usually not appropriate from a time and energy standpoint. Discuss this with students before the visit. If someone makes this type of request, the escort will need to remind the students of the agreement to autograph books only. The author/illustrator should not be put in the position of having to refuse children's requests. To prevent this problem, you could ask the author/illustrator to write an autographed message on a piece of school stationery. With permission, you could duplicate it for all students.

## AFTER THE VISIT

Conclude the author/illustrator focus unit by writing thank-you notes and discussing the special events of the day. The chair of the planning committee should follow up to make sure honorarium payments and expense reimbursements have been made promptly. Unless other arrangements are made, the honorarium should be given to the author/illustrator at the conclusion of the day. Initiate the paperwork for reimbursing expenses as soon as possible after the author's/illustrator's departure.

Though it's not required, sending the author/illustrator your personal letter of thanks and including a picture or two of the day's events is a gesture that almost everyone appreciates. Enlarge a favorite picture of the author/illustrator during the visit to frame and put in an "author's gallery" as a lasting memento of the day.

## FORM 12 — SAMPLE FLOOR PLAN FOR BOOK SALES

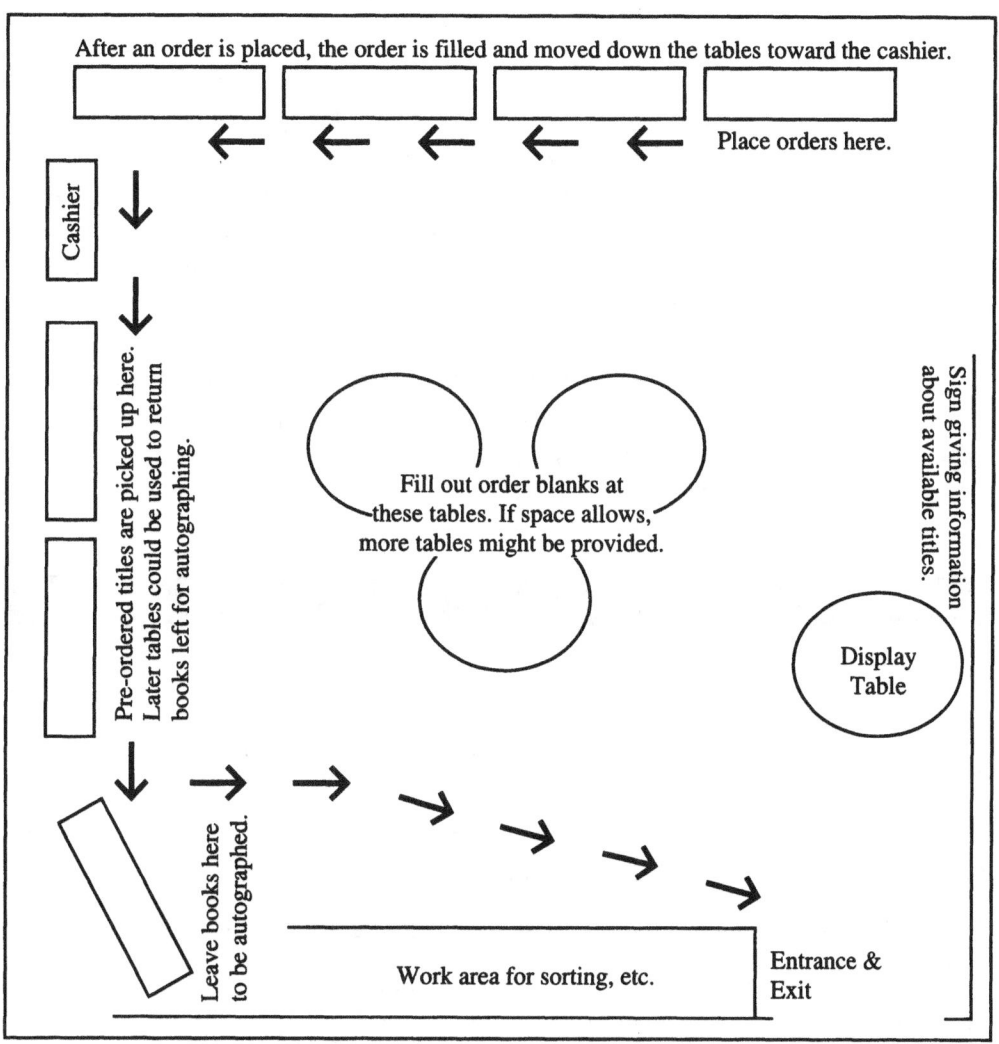

**FORM 13** SAMPLE BOOK ORDER FOR AN AUTHOR/ILLUSTRATOR VISIT

# Loreen Leedy to Visit Van Buren Elementary
# Friday, March 16

On March 16, 2001, our school will host a visit by author Loreen Leedy. Your child will have an opportunity to meet the author, hear her speak, ask questions, and have books autographed. We would like to offer the opportunity to purchase books by Loreen Leedy. **Books need to be ordered early to ensure that we have them for autographing during the author's visit. Prices on this sheet represent a 10 percent discount for ordered and prepaid books. After March 1, any books still available will be at list price.** If you or your child would like to purchase any of the following books, please fill out the order coupon and return **with your payment** to your child's classroom teacher by February 28, 2001. Make checks payable to: Van Buren PTO.

| QTY | TITLE | PRICE | TOTAL |
|---|---|---|---|
| | Books written and illustrated by Loreen Leedy | | |
| _____ | Subtraction Action | $_____ | $_____ |
| _____ | Mission Addition | $_____ | $_____ |
| _____ | Mapping Penny's World | $_____ | $_____ |
| _____ | Measuring Penny | $_____ | $_____ |
| _____ | The Edible Pyramid | $_____ | $_____ |
| _____ | Messages in the Mailbox | $_____ | $_____ |
| _____ | Celebrate 50 States | $_____ | $_____ |
| | | **TOTAL $** | _____ |

Child's name: _____

Teacher's name: _____ Room # _____

Return order and payment to: Van Buren Elementary by February 28, 2001
**Check for the total amount should be payable to: Van Buren PTO.**

## FORM 14 — AUTOGRAPH FORMS FOR SCHOOL VISITS

**AUTOGRAPHING REQUEST**

Your Name: _____
Teacher's name: _____
Room # _____
Title of book: _____

Check one:
- ☐ Signature only.
- ☐ Date and signature.
- ☐ Date, signature, and inscription to:

_____
(Print name as it should be put in the book.)

---- *cut here* ----

**AUTOGRAPHING REQUEST**

Your Name: _____
Teacher's name: _____
Room # _____
Title of book: _____

Check one:
- ☐ Signature only.
- ☐ Date and signature.
- ☐ Date, signature, and inscription to:

_____
(Print name as it should be put in the book.)

---- *cut here* ----

**AUTOGRAPHING REQUEST**

Your Name: _____
Teacher's name: _____
Room # _____
Title of book: _____

Check one:
- ☐ Signature only.
- ☐ Date and signature.
- ☐ Date, signature, and inscription to:

_____
(Print name as it should be put in the book.)

---- *cut here* ----

**AUTOGRAPHING REQUEST**

Your Name: _____
Teacher's name: _____
Room # _____
Title of book: _____

Check one:
- ☐ Signature only.
- ☐ Date and signature.
- ☐ Date, signature, and inscription to:

_____
(Print name as it should be put in the book.)

**FORM 15** — AUTOGRAPH FORMS FOR NON-SCHOOL VISITS

---

**AUTOGRAPHING REQUEST**

Your Name: _____

Address: _____

Title of book: _____

Check one:
- ☐ Signature only.
- ☐ Date and signature.
- ☐ Date, signature, and inscription to: _____

(Print name as it should be put in the book.)

---

**AUTOGRAPHING REQUEST**

Your Name: _____

Address: _____

Title of book: _____

Check one:
- ☐ Signature only.
- ☐ Date and signature.
- ☐ Date, signature, and inscription to: _____

(Print name as it should be put in the book.)

---

*cut here*

---

**AUTOGRAPHING REQUEST**

Your Name: _____

Address: _____

Title of book: _____

Check one:
- ☐ Signature only.
- ☐ Date and signature.
- ☐ Date, signature, and inscription to: _____

(Print name as it should be put in the book.)

---

**AUTOGRAPHING REQUEST**

Your Name: _____

Address: _____

Title of book: _____

Check one:
- ☐ Signature only.
- ☐ Date and signature.
- ☐ Date, signature, and inscription to: _____

(Print name as it should be put in the book.)

# Resources

Finding a video for use or purchase demands some effort. Within the past few years several video producers have disappeared from the scene. Trumpet Book Clubs, which produced several great author videos, was eventually purchased by Scholastic. Some of those videos are still available through Weston Woods, another video producer purchased by Scholastic. American School Publishers, which, for a time, was the source for many excellent author/illustrator videos, was first merged into the SRA/McGraw-Hill Company and now seems to have ceased to exist. However, some of the videos American School Publishers produced are currently available through video distribution firms.

Complicating the situation is that many distributors do not list the original producer or distributor; often the copyright date is missing or inaccurate. Titles for what may be the same video are slightly different when listed by different distributors. Some omit the series title; others do not use the complete title. Library Video <http://www.libraryvideo.com> and Communication Skills <http://www.communicationskills.com/> as well as AIMS <http://www.aims-multimedia.com> are suppliers of author videos. Scholastic lists some of Weston Woods' videos on the Scholastic site at <http://www.scholastic.com>.

Information about videos is difficult to decipher. It is almost impossible to ascertain if an "old" video is the same as one currently offered. There may be sources that I do not know about that offer some of the older videos for sale. For that reason, I am including a retrospective list of videos that no longer seem to be available but that may be available in public or school libraries. Possibly a distributor not listed here will have the video you are looking for.

Following the retrospective list, I list titles which I have ascertained as being available in 2001. In this current list, whenever possible I have tried to list the producer rather than a distributor as the source. The most up-to-date editions will be available from the original producer, but distributors may have out-of-stock or out-of-print videos no longer available from a producer. In one instance, a distributor still makes available an out-of-date video that has subsequently been updated by the producer. But another distributor has a sought-after edition of a video produced by the now defunct American School Publishers. *Caveat emptor*—Let the buyer beware!

In the list of books about authors/illustrators, I have included collective resources as well as selected individual titles. For the most part, I have not included books for adults about individual authors but only biographies for young readers. These books may or may not be in print at the time of this book's publication. Check with a current edition of *Books in Print* if you wish to purchase a title, or check your library or a nearby library for a copy you may borrow.

As with videos, it is important to note the copyright date of the book as the information can only be as current as the date it was written—often a year or so before the publication date.

I have included resources that might help you plan a successful author/illustrator day in your community. Many of them will give background information about various authors and illustrators. Other sources will provide prototypes for author/illustrator focus units and related activities for integrating literature into other curricular areas. Enjoy learning more about your favorite author/illustrator and enjoy your next author/illustrator visit—in person, via video, by telephone, or through the mails.

## VIDEOS ABOUT AUTHORS AND ILLUSTRATORS

The video titles on the following lists have been, and many still are, available for purchase. All of them might be available in local libraries. Since some of the subjects of the videos listed below are no longer living (Ezra Jack Keats, James Marshall, Dr. Seuss, and others) or do not make school visits (Eric Carle, Bill Peet, and others), those videos will not be useful for acquainting young readers with the subject prior to a visit, but they will serve to acquaint young readers with these authors/illustrators and to compare their lives and work with others'. They may also be part of the activities for an author visit or focus that will culminate in another type of activity. The lists are alphabetized by subject.

### RETROSPECTIVE LIST

Brown, Marc. *Meet Marc Brown*. American School Publishers, 1991.

Bryan, Ashley. *Meet Ashley Bryan: Storyteller, Artist, Writer*. American School Publishers, 1991.

Bunting, Eve. *A Visit with Eve Bunting*. Houghton Mifflin/Clarion, 1991.

Burch, Jennings Michael. *Good Conversation! A Talk with Jennings Michael Burch*. Tom Podell, 1991.

Calhoun, Mary. *The Making of a Storybook: Mary Calhoun, Storyteller*. Chip Taylor, 1991.

Cherry, Lynne. *Get to Know Lynne Cherry*. Harcourt Brace, 1993.

Crews, Donald. *Trumpet Video Visits Donald Crews*. Trumpet Club, 1992.

Daugherty, James. *James Daugherty*. Weston Woods, 1972.

Freedman, Russell. *A Visit with Russell Freedman*. Houghton Mifflin/Clarion, 1990.

Fritz, Jean. *Jean Fritz*. Putnam and Grosset, 1986.

Gay, Marie-Louise. *Meet the Author: Marie-Louise Gay*. Clearvue, 1991.

Godfrey, Martyn. *Meet the Author: Martyn Godfrey*. Clearvue, 1991.

Gorman, Carol. *Celebrating Authors: Meet Carol Gorman*. Hi Willow, 1992.

Gryski, Camilla. *Meet the Author: Camilla Gryski*. Clearvue, 1991.

Halvorson, Marilyn. *Meet the Author: Marilyn Halvorson*. Clearvue, 1991.

Jukes, Mavis. *The Writing Process: A Conversation with Mavis Jukes*. Coronet/MTI, 1989.

Keats, Ezra Jack. *Ezra Jack Keats*. Weston Woods, 1973.

Korman, Gordon. *Meet the Author: Gordon Korman*. Clearvue, 1991.

Kuskin, Karla. *Good Conversation! A Talk with Karla Kuskin*. Tom Podell, 1991.

L'Engle, Madeleine. *Madeleine L'Engle: Star*Gazer*. Ishtar Films, 1989.

Little, Jean. *Meet the Author: Jean Little*. Clearvue, 1987.

Lowry, Lois. *A Visit with Lois Lowry*. Houghton Mifflin, 1985.

Lowry, Lois. *Lois Lowry*. Profiles in Literature, 1990.

Macaulay, David. *David Macaulay in His Studio*. Houghton Mifflin, 1981.

Marshall, James. *James Marshall in His Studio*. Houghton Mifflin, 1987.

Martin, Jacqueline Briggs. *Celebrating Authors: Meet Jacqueline Briggs Martin*. Hi Willow, 1992.

McCloskey, Robert. *Robert McCloskey*. Weston Woods, 1965.

Mowat, Farley. *Meet the Author: Farley Mowat*. Clearvue, 1986.

Munsch, Robert. *Meet the Author: Robert Munsch*. Clearvue, 1986.

Naylor, Phyllis Reynolds. *Good Conversation! A Talk with Phyllis Reynolds Naylor*. Tom Podell, 1991. This title has been updated (1999). See current list of videos.

O'Dell, Scott. *A Visit with Scott O'Dell*. Houghton Mifflin, 1983.

Paterson, Katherine. *The Author's Eye: Katherine Paterson*. American School Publishers, 1988.

Paulsen, Gary. *Trumpet Video Visits Gary Paulsen*. Trumpet Club, 1992.

Peet, Bill. *Bill Peet in His Studio*. Houghton Mifflin, 1982.

Ringgold, Faith. *Faith Ringgold*. Random House/Crown, 1991.

Sendak, Maurice. *Maurice Sendak*. Weston Woods, 1965 (1986).

Seuss, Dr., see Geisel, Theodor Seuss.

Shaw, Janet. *Meet Janet Shaw*. Pleasant, 1991.

Speare, Elizabeth George. *A Visit with Elizabeth George Speare*. Houghton Mifflin, 1986.

Terban, Marvin. *A Visit with Marvin Terban*. Houghton Mifflin, 1991.

Tripp, Valerie. *Meet Valerie Tripp*. Pleasant, 1991.

Ungerer, Tomi. *Tomi Ungerer: Storyteller*. Weston Woods, 1981.

Voigt, Cynthia. *Cynthia Voigt*. Profiles in Literature, 1988.

Waber, Bernard. *A Visit with Bernard Waber*. Houghton Mifflin, 1992.

Yee, Paul. *Meet the Author: Paul Yee*. Clearvue, 1991.

## CURRENT LIST OF AUTHOR/ILLUSTRATOR VIDEOS

Adler, David. *Good Conversations! A Talk with David Adler*. (2000) Grades 3-8. 20 minutes. Tom Podell Productions. $49.98.

Aliki. See Brandenberg, Aliki.

Andersen, Hans Christian. *Hans Christian Andersen*. (1952) 112 minutes. Library Video Company. Order number K1071. $14.95. Narrated by Danny Kaye. Grades 1-6.

Andersen, Hans Christian. *Meet the Author: Hans Christian Andersen*. (No date given.) Grades 4-8. 15 minutes. Communications Skills. Order number EA-252. $58.

Angelou, Maya. *Intimate Portrait: Maya Angelou* (1996). Grades 6-Adult. 60 minutes. Library Video Company. Order number Y0301. $9.95. Narrated by Oprah Winfrey.

Avi. *Good Conversations! A Talk with Avi*. (1995) Tom Podell Productions. 22 minutes. Grades 3-8. $49.98.

Babbitt, Natalie. *Good Conversations! A Talk with Natalie Babbitt*. (1995) Tom Podell Productions. 20 minutes. Grades 3-8. $49.98.

Banks, Lynne Reid. *Good Conversations! A Talk with Lynne Reid Banks*. (1995) Tom Podell Productions. 22 minutes. Grades 3-8. $49.98.

Baum, L. Frank. *The Real, the True, the Gen-u-ine Wizard of Oz: L. Frank Baum* (No date given.) Grades 5-8. . Communications Skills. Order number EA-274. $58.

Berenstain, Stan and Jan Berenstain. *Meet Stan and Jan Berenstain* (No date given.) Grades 3-6. 13 minutes. Communications Skills. Order number EA-244. $54.

Bradfield, Jolly Roger. *Creating a Children's Book*.

(1971). Grades K-8. 12 minutes. AIMS. Order number 4115-EN-VID. $49.95.

Brandenberg, Aliki. *Good Conversations! A Talk with Aliki.* (1997) Tom Podell Productions. 20 minutes. Grades 3-8. $49.98.

Bryan, Ashley. *Meet Ashley Bryan: Storyteller, Artist, Writer* (1991) Grades 3-8. 30 minutes. Communications Skills. (No date given.) Order number EA-248. $85. Originally produced and distributed by American School Publishers.

Bunting, Eve. *Good Conversations! A Talk with Eve Bunting.* (2000) Tom Podell Productions. 20 minutes. Grades 3-8. $49.98.

Byars, Betsy. *Good Conversations! A Talk with Betsy Byars.* (1994) Tom Podell Productions. 18 minutes. Grades 3-8. $49.98.

Byars, Betsy. *Meet the Newbery Author: Betsy Byars.* (1991) Grades 3-8. 13 minutes. Communications Skills. Order number EA-245. $54. Originally produced and distributed by American School Publishers.

Carle, Eric. *Eric Carle: Picture Writer.* (1993). Grades K-4. 27 minutes. Library Video Company. Order number Y4406. $39.95. Available from Weston Woods. Order Number QPT880V. $30. Produced by Philomel Publishers in cooperation with Scholastic books.

Carroll, Lewis. *Lewis Carroll: Nonsense Poems and Glimmers of Life.* (1989). Grades 7-12. 27 minutes. Library Video Company. Order number Y0004. $44.95.

Christopher, Matthew. *Good Conversations! A Talk with Matt Christopher.* (1994) Tom Podell Productions. 18 minutes. Grades 3-8. $49.98.

Cormier, Robert. *Good Conversations! A Talk with Robert Cormier.* (1996) Tom Podell Productions. 20 minutes. Grades 3-8. $49.98.

Coville, Bruce. *Good Conversations! A Talk with Bruce Coville.* (1993) Tom Podell Productions. 22 minutes. Grades 3-8. $49.98.

Curtis, Christopher Paul. *Good Conversations! A Talk with Christopher Paul Curtis.* (2000) Tom Podell Productions. 20 minutes. Grades 3-8. $49.98.

Dahl, Roald. *The Author's Eye: Roald Dahl*. Author's Notebook/Teacher Resource Book/Full Color Poster. (1988) Grades 4-8. 25 minutes. Communications Skills. Order number EA-269. $138. Originally produced and distributed by American School Publishers.

dePaola, Tomie. *A Visit With Tomie dePaola.* (1996) Grades 5 & up. 25 minutes. Library Video Company. Order number Y4405. $19.95.

dePaola, Tomie. *Tomie dePaola Live in Concert: The Pied Piper of Children's Books.* (1999) Grades 3 & up. 65 minutes. Library Video Company. Order number Y4407. $19.95.

Dorros, Arthur. *Good Conversations! A Talk with Arthur Dorros.* (2000) Tom Podell Productions. 20 minutes. Grades 3-8. $49.98.

Estes, Eleanor. *Meet the Newbery Author: Eleanor Estes* (1991) Grades 3-6. 15 minutes. Communications Skills. Order number EA-246. $54.00. Originally produced and distributed by American School Publishers.

Fleischman, Sid. *Meet the Newbery Author: Sid Fleischman.* (1990). Grades K-6. 20 minutes. AIMS. Order number A32-EN-VID. $59.95.

Fox, Mem. *Trumpet Video Visits Mem Fox.* (1992) Weston Woods. 18 minutes. Grades K-3. $30. Originally produced for Trumpet Video.

Fox, Paula. *Good Conversations! A Talk with Paula Fox* (1992) Tom Podell Productions. 24 minutes. Grades 3-8. $49.98.

Freedman, Russell. *Meet The Newbery Author: Russell Freedman.* (1991) Grades 5-8. . Communications Skills. Order number EA-272. $88. Originally produced and distributed by American School Publishers.

Fritz, Jean. *Good Conversations! A Talk with Jean Fritz.* (1993) Tom Podell Productions. 20 minutes. Grades 3-8. $49.98.

Fritz, Jean. *Jean Fritz: Six Revolutionary War Figures.* (1977). Weston Woods. 31 minutes. Grades 3-6. $39.95. Narrated by Jean Fritz. Introductory comments explain why she wrote the series of American Revolutionary biographies.

Geisel, Theodor Seuss. *Who's Dr. Seuss? Meet Ted Geisel.* (1980) Grades 3-8. 14 minutes. Communications Skills. Order number EA-250. $56. Originally produced and distributed by American School Publishers.

George, Jean Craighead. *Good Conversations! A Talk with Jean Craighead George.* (1991) Tom Podell Productions. 26 minutes. Grades 3-8. $49.98.

George, Jean Craighead. *Meet The Newbery Author: Jean Craighead George.* (1989) Grades 5-8. 17 min-

utes. Communications Skills. Order number EA-273. $54. Originally produced and distributed by American School Publishers.

Giff, Patricia Reilly. *Good Conversations! A Talk with Patricia Reilly Giff.* (1996) Tom Podell Productions. 20 minutes. Grades 3-8. $49.98.

Hamilton, Virginia. *Meet The Newbery Author: Virginia Hamilton.* (No date given.) Grades 4-8.Communications Skills. Order number EA-261. $85. Originally produced and distributed by American School Publishers.

Henry, Marguerite. *Story of a Book* (2nd edition). (1990). Grades 3-8. 16 minutes. AIMS (Pied Piper). Order number PP901V-EN-VID. $49.95. Tells how Marguerite Henry researched and wrote *San Domingo, Medicine Hat Stallion*. Released earlier as a filmstrip cassette. Released in 1990 in video format.

Henry, Marguerite. *Meet The Newbery Author: Marguerite Henry.* (1980) Grades 4-8. 18 minutes. Communications Skills. Order number EA-262. $54. Originally produced and distributed by American School Publishers.

Hesse, Karen. *Good Conversations! A Talk with Karen Hesse.* (1998) Tom Podell Productions. 20 minutes. Grades 3-8. $49.98.

Holling, Hollings C. *Story of a Book, Hollings C. Holling.* (1990). Grades K-6. 11 minutes. AIMS. Order number VSB-EN-VID. $40. Holling discusses the making of *Pagoo*. Released earlier as a filmstrip cassette. Released in 1990 in video format.

Hopkins, Lee Bennett. *Good Conversations! A Talk with Lee Bennett Hopkins.* (1991) Tom Podell Productions. 18 minutes. Grades 3-8. $49.98.

Hurwitz, Johanna. *Good Conversations! A Talk with Johanna Hurwitz.* (1997) Tom Podell Productions. 20 minutes. Grades 3-8. $49.98.

Kellogg, Steven. *Trumpet Video Visits Steven Kellogg.* (1993). Weston Woods. 17 minutes. Grades K-3. $30. Originally produced by Maggie Kneip for Trumpet Video.

Kerr, M. E. *Good Conversations! A Talk with M. E. Kerr.* (1991) Tom Podell Productions. 24 minutes. Grades 3-8. $49.98.

Konigsburg, E. L. *Good Conversations! A Talk with E. L. Konigsburg.* (1995). Tom Podell Productions. 22 minutes. Grades 3-8. $49.98

L'Engle, Madeleine. *Good Conversations! A Talk with Madeleine L'Engle.* (1994) Tom Podell Productions. 22 minutes. Grades 3-8. $49.98.

L'Engle, Madeleine. *Meet The Newbery Author: Madeleine L'Engle.* (date unknown) Grades 4-8. 16 minutes. Communications Skills. Order number EA-263. $54. Originally produced and distributed by American School Publishers.

Lewis, C. S. *The Life of C. S. Lewis: Through Joy and Beyond.* (1979). Grades 7-12. 60 minutes. Library Video Company. Order number Y0001. $12.95.

Lionni, Leo. *Meet Leo Lionni* (1992) Grades 4-8. 20 minutes. Communications Skills. Order number EA-258. $85. Originally produced and distributed by American School Publishers.

Lisle, Janet Taylor. *Meet Janet Taylor Lisle.* (No date given.) Grades 4-8. 28 minutes. Communications Skills. Order number EA-259. $85.

Lobel, Arnold. *Meet The Newbery Author: Arnold Lobel* (1991) Grades 4-8. 12 minutes. Communications Skills. Order number EA-264. $54. Originally produced and distributed by American School Publishers.

Martin, Bill, Jr. *A Visit with Bill Martin, Jr.* (1996). Weston Woods. 26 minutes. Grades 3-5. $29.95. Originally produced by Henry Holt and Company.

McDaniel, Lurlene. *Good Conversations! A Talk with Lurlene McDaniel.* (1997) Tom Podell Productions. 22 minutes. Grades 3-8. $49.98.

McDermott, Gerald. *Get to Know Gerald McDermott.* (1994) Grades 2-6. 20 minutes. Weston Woods. Order number QHA885V. $40.00. Produced by Harcourt Brace & Company.

McGovern, Ann. *Good Conversations! A Talk with Ann McGovern.* (1991) Tom Podell Productions. 24 minutes. Grades 3-8. $49.98.

McKinley, Robin. *Good Conversations! A Talk with Robin McKinley.* (1997) Tom Podell Productions. 20 minutes. Grades 3-8. $49.98.

McKissack, Fredrick and Patricia McKissack. *Good Conversations! A Talk with the McKissacks.* (1997) Tom Podell Productions. 20 minutes. Grades 3-8. $49.98.

Most, Bernard. *Get to Know Bernard Most.* (1993) Harcourt Brace, 20 minutes. Grades K-4. Catalog number #0-15-253159-9.

Naylor, Phyllis Reynolds. *Good Conversations! A Talk with Phyllis Reynolds Naylor*, updated edition. (1999) Tom Podell Productions. 20 minutes. Grades 3-8. $49.98.

Nixon, Joan Lowery. *Good Conversations! A Talk with Joan Lowery Nixon*. (1996) Tom Podell Productions. 20 minutes. Grades 3-8. $49.98.

O'Dell, Scott. *Meet The Newbery Author: Scott O'Dell* (1991) Grades 4-8. 14 minutes. Communications Skills. Order number EA-265. $56. Originally produced and distributed by American School Publishers.

Paterson, Katherine. *The Author's Eye: Katherine Paterson*. Teacher Resource Book/25 Author's Notebooks, Full Color Poster. (1991) Grades 4-8. 25 minutes. Communications Skills. Order number EA-268. $207. Originally produced and distributed by American School Publishers.

Paterson, Katherine. *Good Conversations! A Talk with Katherine Paterson*. (1999) Tom Podell Productions. 20 minutes. Grades 3-8. $49.98.

Peck, Richard. *Good Conversations! A Talk with Richard Peck*. (1997) Tom Podell Productions. 20 minutes. Grades 3-8. $49.98.

Peck, Robert Newton. *Good Conversations! A Talk with Robert Newton Peck*. Tom Podell Productions. 20 minutes. Grades 3-8. $49.98.

Pinkney, Jerry. *A Visit with Jerry Pinkney*. (1997). Grades 2-5. 25 minutes. Weston Woods. $29.95. Originally produced and distributed by Dial Books for Young Readers.

Pinkney, Jerry. *Meet the Caldecott Illustrator: Jerry Pinkney* (1991) Grades 4-8. 21 minutes. Communications Skills. Order number EA-256. $585. Originally produced and distributed by American School Publishers.

Polacco, Patricia. *Patricia Polacco: Dream Keeper*. (1996) Grades 1-5. 23 minutes. Library Video Company. Order number K1583. $39.95.

Potok, Chaim. *Good Conversations! A Talk with Chaim Potok*. (1997) Tom Podell Productions. 20 minutes. Grades 3-8. $49.98.

Potter, Beatrix. *Beatrix Potter: A Private World*. (1973). Grade 5 & Up. 42 minutes. Library Video Company. Order number Y1016. $24.95.

Potter, Beatrix. *Beatrix Potter: Artist, Storyteller and Countrywoman*. (1997). Grade 6 & Up. 58 minutes. Library Video Company. Order number Y4401. $29.95. Based on the Potter biography by Judy Taylor (Frederick Warne & Co.) Narrated by Lynn Redgrave.

Prelutsky, Jack. *Meet Jack Prelutsky* (1991) Grades 4-8. 20 minutes. Communications Skills. Order number EA-260. $85. Originally produced and distributed by American School Publishers (SRA/McGraw-Hill).

Rowling, J. K. *The Magical World of Harry Potter: The Unauthorized Story of J. K. Rowling*. (2000). Grade 3 & Up. 48 minutes. Library Video Company. Order number K3088. $9.95. Available as a DVD. Order number V0143. $14.95.

Rylant, Cynthia. *Meet the Author: Cynthia Rylant Video Series*. (1991) Grades 4-8. 30 minutes. Communications Skills. Order number EA-254. $137. Originally produced and distributed by American School Publishers. Contains both the *Meet the Newbery Author* and the *Meet the Picture Book Author* video.

Rylant, Cynthia. *Meet the Newbery Author: Cynthia Rylant*.(1991) Grades 4-8. 20 minutes. Communications Skills. Order number EA-249. $85. Originally produced and distributed by American School Publishers.

Rylant, Cynthia. *Meet the Picture Book Author: Cynthia Rylant*. (1991) Grades 3-8. 10 minutes. Communications Skills. Order number EA-257. $72. Originally produced and distributed by American School Publishers.

Sachar, Louis. *Good Conversations! A Talk with Louis Sachar*. (1999) Tom Podell Productions. 20 minutes. Grades 3-8. $49.98.

Sendak, Maurice. *The Maurice Sendak Library*. (1989) Grades PreK-4. 35 minutes. Library Video Company. Order number 4458. $14.95. A compilation of three films of Sendak's stories. Originally directed by Gene Deitch and produced and distributed by Weston Woods. In the third, Sendak talks about his childhood in an excerpt from a longer video titled *Sendak*.

Seuss, Dr. See Geisel, Theodor Seuss.

Snyder, Zilpha Keatley. *Good Conversations! A Talk with Zilpha Keatley Snyder*. (1998) Tom Podell Productions. 20 minutes. Grades 3-8. $49.98.

Spinelli, Jerry. *Good Conversations! A Talk with Jerry Spinelli*. (1994) Tom Podell Productions. 20 minutes. Grades 3-8. $49.98.

Steig, William. *Getting to Know William Steig.* (1995) Grades 5 & Up. 20 minutes. Weston Woods. $30.

Taylor, Mildred. *Meet The Newbery Author: Mildred D. Taylor* (1991) Grades 4-8. 21 minutes. Communications Skills. Order number EA-266. $85. Originally produced and distributed by American School Publishers.

Taylor, Theodore. *Good Conversations! A Talk with Theodore Taylor.* (1998) Tom Podell Productions. 20 minutes. Grades 3-8. $49.98.

Tudor, Tasha. *Take Joy! The Magical World of Tasha Tudor.* (1997) All ages. 47 minutes. Library Video Company. Order number Y4404. $29.95. Also available from Scholastic. Order number WMPV446. $30. Produced and directed by Sarah Kerruish for Spellbound Productions, in association with Corgi Cottage Industries.

Wells, Rosemary. *A Visit With Rosemary Wells.* (1997) Grade 6 & Up. 30 minutes. Weston Woods. $30.00. Originally produced by Penguin Publishers.

Wilder, Laura Ingalls. *Meet The Newbery Author: Laura Ingalls Wilder* (1991) Grades 4-8. 18 minutes. Communications Skills. Order number EA-267. $54. Originally produced and distributed by American School Publishers.

Willard, Nancy. *Good Conversations! A Talk with Nancy Willard.* (1991) Tom Podell Productions. 18 minutes. Grades 3-8. $49.98.

Yep, Laurence. *Good Conversations! A Talk with Laurence Yep.* (1998) Tom Podell Productions. 20 minutes. Grades 3-8. $49.98.

Yolen, Jane. *Good Conversations! A Talk with Jane Yolen.* (1997) Tom Podell Productions. 22 minutes. Grades 3-8. $49.98.

## BOOKS ABOUT AUTHORS AND ILLUSTRATORS

The titles in the following list are among the most comprehensive in terms of information about authors and illustrators of children's and young adult literature. These are reference sources whose major purpose is to give information about authors/illustrators. I have included selected titles that focus on just one author or illustrator if it was intended for a young reader audience.

*The Art of Eric Carle.* Philomel, 1996.

*Book Report & Library Talk Author Profile Collection.* Compiled by the Editors of *The Book Report* and *Library Talk*. Professional Growth Series. Linworth Publishing, 1992.

Byars, Betsy. *The Moon and I.* Messner, 1992.

*Children's Literature Review.* Gale, 1976- (Series).

Cummings, Pat, editor. *Talking with Artists, Vol. 3: Conversations with Peter Catalanotto, Raul Colon, Lisa Desimini, Jane Dyer, Kevin Hawkes, G. Brian Karas, Betsy Lewin, Ted Lewin, Keiko Narahashi, Elise Primavera, Anna Rich, Peter Sis, and Paul O. Zelinsky.* Houghton Mifflin, 1999.

Cummings, Pat, editor. *Talking With Artists, Volume 2: Conversations with Thomas B. Allen, Mary Jane Begin, Floyd Cooper, Julie Downing, Denise Fleming, Sheila Hamanaka, Kevin Henkes, William Joyce, Maira Kalman, Deborah Nourse Lattimore, Brian Pinkney, Vera B. Williams, and David Wisniewski.* Simon & Schuster, 1995.

Cummings, Pat, editor. *Talking with Artists. Victoria Chess, Pat Cummings, Leo and Diane Dillon, Richard Egielski, Lois Ehlert, Lisa Campbell Ernst, Tom Feelings, Steven Kellogg, Jerry Pinkney, Amy Schwartz, Lane Smith, Chris Van Allsburg, and David Wiesner.* Simon & Schuster, 1992.

de Montreville, Doris and Elizabeth D. Crawford, eds. *Fourth Book of Junior Authors & Illustrators.* H. W. Wilson, 1978.

de Montreville, Doris and Donna Hill, eds. *Third Book of Junior Authors*. H. W. Wilson, 1972.

Drew, Bernard A. *The 100 most popular young adult authors: biographical sketches and bibliographies*. Rev. 1st Ed. Libraries Unlimited, 1997.

*Elementary Author/Illustrator Profiles*. Compiled by the Editors of *The Book Report* and *Library Talk*. Professional Growth Series. Linworth Publishing, 1996.

Fletcher, Marilyn P. and James L. Thorson, compilers. *Reader's Guide to Twentieth-Century Science Fiction*. American Library Association, 1989.

Fuller, Muriel, ed. *More Junior Authors*. H. W. Wilson, 1963.

Helbig, Alethea K. and Agnes Regan Perkins. *Dictionary of American Children's Fiction*, 1960-1984. Greenwood, 1986.

Hoffman, Miriam and Eva Samuels. *Authors and Illustrators of Children's Books*. R. R. Bowker, 1974.

Holtz, Sally Holmes, ed. *Fifth Book of Junior Authors & Illustrators*. H. W. Wilson, 1983.

Holtz, Sally Holmes, ed. *Sixth Book of Junior Authors & Illustrators*. H. W. Wilson, 1989.

Holtz, Sally Holmes, ed. *Seventh Book of Junior Authors & Illustrators*. H. W. Wilson, 1996.

Marcus, Leonard S. and Judy Blume, editors. *Author Talk: Conversations With Judy Blume, Bruce Brooks, Karen Cushman, Russell Freedman, Lee Bennett Hopkins, James Howe, Johanna Hurwitz, E. L. Konigsburg*. Simon & Schuster, 2000.

McElmeel, Sharron L. *100 Most Popular Children's Authors: Biographical Sketches and Bibliographies*. Libraries Unlimited, 1999.

McElmeel, Sharron L. *100 Most Popular Picture Book Authors and Illustrators: Biographical Sketches and Bibliographies*. Libraries Unlimited, 2000.

McElmeel, Sharron L. *An Author a Month (for Dimes)*. Libraries Unlimited/TIP, 1992.

McElmeel, Sharron L. *An Author a Month (for Nickels)*. Libraries Unlimited/TIP, 1990.

McElmeel, Sharron L. *An Author a Month (for Pennies)*. Libraries Unlimited, 1988.

McElmeel, Sharron L. *Authors for Children: A Calendar*. Hi Willow, 1992.

McElmeel, Sharron L. *Bookpeople: A First Album*. Libraries Unlimited/TIP, 1990.

McElmeel, Sharron L. *Bookpeople: A Multicultural Album*. Libraries Unlimited/TIP, 1992

McElmeel, Sharron L. *Bookpeople: A Second Album*. Libraries Unlimited/TIP, 1990.

McElmeel, Sharron L. *The Poet Tree*. Libraries Unlimited/TIP, 1993.

Peck, Richard. *Anonymously Yours*. Messner, 1992.

Peet, Bill. *Bill Peet: An Autobiography*. Houghton Mifflin, 1989.

Ringgold, Faith. *Dancing at the Louvre: Faith Ringgold's French Collection and Other Story Quilts*. University of California Press, 1998.

Rockman, Connie. *The Eighth Book of Junior Authors and Illustrators*. H. W. Wilson, 2000.

Roginski, Jim. *Behind the Covers, Vol. 2*. Libraries Unlimited, 1989.

Roginski, Jim. *Behind the Covers*. Libraries Unlimited, 1985.

Roginski, Jim. *Newbery and Caldecott Medalists and Honor Book Winners*. Libraries Unlimited, 1982.

*Something About the Author*. Gale, 1976- (Series).

Stanley J. Kunitz and Howard Haycraft, eds. *The Junior Book of Authors*. H. W. Wilson, 1951.

*Twentieth-Century Children's Writers*. 3rd ed. St. James Press, 1989.

*Twentieth-Century Children's Writers*. St. Martin's Press, 1978.

Uchida, Yoshiko. *The Invisible Thread*. Messner, 1992.

Ward, Martha E. and Dorothy A. Marquardt, *Authors of Books for Young People*, 2nd ed. Scarecrow Press, 1971.

## SELECTED SOURCES OF AUTHOR VIDEOS

AIMS Multimedia
9710 DeSoto Avenue
Chatsworth, CA 91311
(800) 367-2467, ext. 448
http://www.aims-multimedia.com

Communications Skills, Inc.
49 Richmondville Ave
Westport, CT 06880
(800) 824-2398
(203) 226-8820 fax
http://store.yahoo.com/cskills/index.html

Library Video Company
7 E. Wynnewood Road
Wynnewood, PA 19096
(800) 843-3620
http://www.libraryvideo.com

Tim Podell Productions
P. O. Box 244
Scarborough, NY 10510
(800) 642-4181; fax (914) 944-8110
http://www.goodconversations.com

Weston Woods
265 Post Road West
Westport, CT 06880
(800) 243-5020; fax (203) 222-1009

## SELECTED SOURCES OF CHILDREN'S AND YOUNG ADULT LITERATURE AND RESOURCES ABOUT AUTHORS AND ILLUSTRATORS

Atheneum Books for Young People
230 Avenue of the Americas
New York, NY 10020
(212) 698-7200
Imprint of Simon and Schuster
<http://www.simonsays.com>

Albert Whitman and Co.
6340 Oakton St.
Morton Grove, IL 60053-2723
(847) 581-0033
<http://www.albertwhitman.com/>

August House Littlefolk
P. O. Box 3223
Little Rock, AR 72203-3223
(501) 372-5450; fax (501) 372-5579
<http://www.augusthouse.com>

Avon Books
1350 Avenue of the Americas
New York, NY 10019
(212) 261-6800
Imprint of HarperCollins
<http://www.harpercollins.com>

Bantam Doubleday Dell Books for Young Readers
1540 Broadway
New York, NY 10036
(212) 354-6500
Imprint of Random House Publishers
<http://www.randomhouse.com/>

Beech Tree Books
1350 Avenue of the Americas
New York, NY 10019
(212) 261-6500
Imprint of HarperCollins
<http://www.harpercollins.com>

Blue Sky Press
555 Broadway
New York, NY 10012-3999
(212) 343-6100
Imprint of Scholastic Press
<http://www.scholastic.com>

CarolRhoda Books, Inc.
241 First Avenue North
Minneapolis, MN 55401
(612) 332-3344
(800) 328-4929

Candlewick Press
2067 Massachusetts Avenue
Cambridge, MA 02140
(617) 661-3330
<http://www.candlewick.com/>

Charlesbridge Publishing
85 Main Street
Watertown, MA 02172
(617) 926-0329
<http://www.charlesbridge.com/>

Clarion Books
215 Park Avenue South
New York, NY 10003
(212) 420-5800
Imprint of Houghton Mifflin Publishers
<http://www.houghtonmifflinbooks.com/>

Cobblehill Books
375 Hudson Street
New York, NY 10014
(212) 366-2000

Crown Publishers
201 East 50th Street
New York, NY 10022
(212) 751-2600
Imprint of Random House Publishers
<http://www.randomhouse.com/>

Dial Books for Young Readers
375 Hudson Street
New York, NY 10014
(212) 366-2800
Imprint of Penguin USA, Inc.
<http://www.penguinputnam.com>

DK Publishing, Inc.
95 Madison Avenue
New York, NY 10016
(212) 213-4800

Dutton Children's Books
375 Hudson Street
New York, NY 10014
(212) 366-2527
Imprint of Penguin USA, Inc.
<http://www.penguinputnam.com>

Farrar, Straus & Giroux, Inc.
19 Union Square West
New York, NY 10003
(212) 741-6900

Frederick Warne
375 Hudson Street
New York, NY 10014
(212) 366-2800
Imprint of Penguin USA, Inc.
<http://www.penguinputnam.com>

Greenwillow Books
10 East 53rd Street
New York, NY 10022
(212) 207-7000
Imprint of HarperCollins
<http://www.harpercollins.com>

Harcourt, Inc.
525 B Street, Suite 1900
San Diego, CA 92101
(619) 699-6435
(800) 543-1918
<http://www.harcourtbooks.com/>

HarperCollins Children's Books
includes Greenwillow imprint
10 East 53rd Street
New York, NY 10022
(212) 207-7000
<http://www.harpercollins.com>

Holiday House
425 Madison Avenue
New York, NY 10017
(212) 688-0085
<http://www.holidayhouse.com/>

Henry Holt and Company, Inc.
115 West 18th Street
New York, NY 10011
(212) 886-9200
fax (212) 633-0748
<http://www.henryholt.com>

Houghton Mifflin Co.
222 Berkeley Street
Boston, MA 02116
(617) 351-5000
<http://www.houghtonmifflinbooks.com/>

Hyperion Books for Children
114 Fifth Avenue
New York, NY 10011
(212) 633-4400
<http://www.disney.com>

Just Us Books
356 Glenwood Avenue
East Orange, NJ 07017
(201) 676-4345

Alfred A. Knopf, Inc.
201 East 50th Street
New York, NY 10022
(212) 940-7608
Imprint of Random House Publishers
<http://www.randomhouse.com/>

Lee & Low Books
95 Madison Avenue
New York, NY 10016
(212) 779-4400
<http://www.leeandlow.com/>

Lerner Publications Company
241 First Avenue North
Minneapolis, MN 55401
(612) 332-3344
<http://www.lernerbooks.com/>

Libraries Unlimited, Inc.
P.O. Box 6633
Englewood, CO 80155-6633
(800) 237-6124
<http://www.lu.com>

Linworth Publishing, Inc.
480 E. Wilson Bridge Rd, Suite L.
Worthington, OH 43085-2372
(800) 786-5017
<http://www.linworth.com>

Little, Brown & Co.
34 Beacon Street
Boston, MA 02108
(617) 227-0730
An Imprint of Time Warner
<http://www.twbookmark.com/>

Lodestar Books
375 Hudson Street
New York, NY 10014
(212) 366-2527
Imprint of Penguin USA, Inc.
<http://www.penguinputnam.com>

Margaret K. McElderry Books
1230 Avenue of the Americas
New York, NY 10020
(212) 698-7200
A division of Simon and Schuster, Inc.
Simon & Schuster Children's Publishing
<http://www.simonsays.com/>

The Millbrook Press, Inc.
2 Old New Milford Road
Brookfield, CT 06804
(203) 740-2220
<http://www.millbrookpress.com>

North-South Books
1123 Broadway
Suite 800
New York, NY 10010
(212) 463-9736
<http://www.northsouth.com>

Orchard Books
95 Madison Avenue
New York, NY 10016
(212) 686-7070
An Imprint of Grolier Publishing
<http://www.publishing.grolier.com/>

Peachtree Publishers, Ltd.
494 Armour Circle NE
Atlanta, GA 30324-4088
(404) 876-8761
<http://www.peachtree-online.com>

Pelican Publishing Company Inc.
P.O. Box 3110
Gretna, LA 70054
(504) 368-1175
<http://pelicanpub.com/homepg.htm>

Philomel Books
200 Madison Avenue
New York, NY 10022
(212) 951-8473
Imprint of Penguin USA, Inc.
<http://www.penguinputnam.com>

G.P. Putnam's Sons
200 Madison Avenue
New York, NY 10022
(212) 951-8473
Imprint of Penguin USA, Inc.
<http://www.penguinputnam.com>

Random House
201 East 50th Street
New York, NY 10022
(212) 751-2600
<http://www.random.com>

Richard C. Owen Publishers, Inc.
P. O. Box 585
Katonah, NY 10536
<http://www.rcowens.com>

Scholastic, Inc.
555 Broadway
New York, NY 10012
(212) 343-6100
<http://www.scholastic.com>

Simon and Schuster Books for Young Readers
1230 Avenue of the Americas
New York, NY 10020
(212) 698-7200
Simon & Schuster Children's Publishing
<http://www.simonsays.com/>

Stemmer House Publishers, Inc.
2627 Caves Road
Owings Mills, MD 21117
(410) 363-3690; fax (410) 363-8459
<http://www.stemmer.com>

Viking
375 Hudson Street
New York, NY 10014
(212) 366-2000
Imprint of Penguin USA, Inc.
<http://www.penguinputnam.com>

Walker & Company
435 Hudson Street
New York, NY 10014
(212) 727-8300

## WORLD WIDE WEB AUTHOR/ILLUSTRATOR RESOURCES

The World Wide Web is a fluid resource. Many publishers' sites have information about authors and illustrators, as do general sites such as David K. Brown's Children's Literature Site and university sites that index links to information about authors of children's and young adult literature. In the following lists, I have included several gateways to various author/illustrator sites maintained by the artist or by a fan. Sites with author/illustrator information are not included if they are articles or interviews in another site. For instance, Amazon.com has many author interviews; some school sites, such as the Harrison Elementary School's (Cedar Rapids, Iowa) at <http://www.cr.k12.ia.us/ harr/index.htm>, include pages about recent author visits to the school.

### GATEWAYS TO INFORMATION ABOUT AUTHORS AND ILLUSTRATORS ON THE WEB

Authors on the Web
<http://www.people.Virginia.EDU/~jbh/author.html>

Books@Random Authors on the Web
<www.randomhouse.com/author/links.html>

Children's Authors on the Web
<http://www.frsd.k12.nj.us/barleylibrary/library/author.htm>

David K. Brown's Children's Literature Guide: Authors on the Web    <www.ucalgary.ca/~dkbrown/authors.html>

de Grummond's Children's Literature Collection at the University of Southern Mississippi
<http://www.lib.usm.edu/~degrum/>

Index to Children's Books Authors and Illustrators
<http://falcon.jmu.edu/~ramseyil/biochildhome.htm>

### AUTHOR/ILLUSTRATOR WEB SITES

Arnold, Caroline
<http://www.geocities.com/Athens/1264/>

Arnold, Tedd <http://www.geocities.com/~teddarnold/>

Avi <http://www.avi-writer.com>

Aylesworth, Jim <http://www.ayles.com>

Balgassi, Haemi <http://home.sprynet.com/~balgassi/>

Bang, Molly <http://www.mollybang.com/>

Bellairs, John C. <http://www.compleatbellairs.com/>

Berenstain, Stan and Jan Berenstain
<http://www.berenstainbears.com>

Blume, Judy <http://www.judyblume.com/>

Brett, Jan <http://www.janbrett.com>

Brown, Craig McFarland
<http://www.geocities.com/craigbrown_2000>

Byars, Betsy <http://www.betsybyars.com>

Carle, Eric <http://www.eric-carle.com/>

Carlson, Nancy <http://www.nancycarlson.com/>

Casanova, Mary <http://www.marycasanova.com>

Charlip, Remy <http://www.remycharlip.com/>

Cleary, Beverly
<http://www.teleport.com/~krp/cleary.html>

Cobb, Vicki <http://www.vickicobb.com/>

dePaola, Tomie <http://www.tomiedepaola.com>

Dillon, Leo and Diane Dillon
<http://www.best.com/~libros/dillon/>

Duncan, Lois <http://www.iag.net/~barq/lois.html>; a site about her daughter's unsolved murder <http://www.iag.net/~barq/kait.html>

Florczak, Robert
<http://www.audreywood.com/mac_site/friends_clubhouse/florczak/florczak_page/florczak.htm> or
<http://www.audreywood.com/aw_site_pc/friends_clubhouse/florczak/florczak_page/florczak.htm>

Fox, Mem <http://www.memfox.net/>

Geisel, Theodor Seuss (See Dr. Seuss)

George, Jean Craighead
<http://www.jeancraigheadgeorge.com/>

Gibbons, Gail <http://www.gailgibbons.com>

Gorman, Carol <http://www.geocities.com/carolgorman_2000>

Halperin, Wendy Anderson
<http://www.parrett.net/halperin>

Hamilton, Virginia <http://www.virginiahamilton.com/>

Hopkinson, Deborah <http://people.whitman.edu/~hopkinda/>

Hutchins, Pat <http://www.titch.net>

Jacques, Brian <http://www.redwall.org/dave/jacques.html>

Kehret, Peggy <http://users.owt.com/kehretbp/index.html>

Kurtz, Jane. <http://www.janekurtz.com>

L'Engle, Madeleine <http://www.geocities.com/Athens/Acropolis/8838/>

Lasky, Kathryn <http://www.xensei.com/users/newfilm/homelsk.htm>

Leedy, Loreen <http://www.loreenleedy.com>

Lewis. E. B. <http://www.eblewis.com>

Lindgren, Astrid <http://www.interlog.com/~wings/jane/a_lindgren/a_lindgren.html>

Martin, Bill Jr. <http://tiill.com/authors.htm>

Martin, Jacqueline Briggs <http://www.jacquelinebriggsmartin.com>

McDermott, Gerald (Director of Joseph Campbell Foundation) <http://www.jcf.org/>

McKinley, Robin <http://www.sff.net/people/robinmckinley/>

Milne, A. A. <http://chaos.trxinc.com/jmilne/Pooh/>

Most, Bernard. <http://www.bernardmost.com>

Munsch, Robert <http://www.robertmunsch.com/>

Murphy, Shirley Rousseau <http://www.joegrey.com>

Nixon, Joan Lowery <http://members.aol.com/NikkiB5130/JNixon5130.htm>

Oberman, Sheldon <http://www.mbnet.mb.ca/~soberman/>

Paterson, Katherine <http://www.terabithia.com>

Paulsen, Gary <http://www.garypaulsen.com/>

Peck, Robert Newton <http://my.athenet.net/~blahnik/rnpeck/index.htm>

Pilkey, Dav <http://www.pilkey.com>

Polacco, Patricia <http://www.patriciapolacco.com>

Quackenbush, Robert <http://www.rquackenbush.com>

Ringgold, Faith <http://www.artincontext.org/artist/ringgold/>

Ross, Dave <http://www.albany.net/~dross/>

Rubel, Nicole <http://www.nicolerubel.com/>

Ryan, Pam Muñoz <http://www.PamMunozRyan.com/>

Scieszka, Jon <http://www.chucklebait.com/>

Seuss, Dr. <http://www.afn.org/~afn15301/drseuss.html>

Shannon, David <http://www.audreywood.com/mac_site/friends_clubhouse/shannon/dave_page.htm> or <http://www.audreywood.com/aw_site_pc/friends_clubhouse/shannon/dave_page.htm>

Simon, Seymour <http://www.seymoursimon.com/>

Sîs, Peter <http://www.petersistibet.com/>

Skurzynski, Gloria <http://gloriabooks.com>

Smith, Cynthia Leitich <http://www.cynthialeitichsmith.com>

Smith, Lane <http://www.chucklebait.com/>

Smith, Roland <http://www.rolandsmith.com>

Snyder, Zilpha Keatley <http://www.microweb.com/lsnyder/>

Soto, Gary <http://www.garysoto.com/>

Stanley, Diane <http://www.dianestanley.com>

Stevens, Janet <http://www.janetstevens.com>

Taylor, Harriet Peck <http://www.mooseworld.com/taylor.htm>

Teague, Mark <http://www.audreywood.com/mac_site/friends_clubhouse/teague/teague_page/teague_page.htm> or <http://www.audreywood.com/aw_site_pc/friends_clubhouse/teague/teague_page/teague_page.htm>

Tudor, Tasha <http://www.tashatudor.com/>

Wells, Rosemary <http://www.rosemarywells.com/>

Williams, Suzanne <http://www.suzanne-williams.com/>

Wood, Audrey <http://www.audreywood.com/>

Wood, Don <http://www.audreywood.com/mac_site/don_stuff/don_page/don_page.htm> or <http://www.audreywood.com/aw_site_pc/don_stuff/don_page/don_page.htm>

Yolen, Jane <http://www.janeyolen.com/>

# Author/Illustrator Index

## A
Aardema, Verna, 59
Adoff, Arnold, 31
Arnold, Carol, 14
Aruego, José, 60
Avi, 61, 63, 64
Aylesworth, Jim, 30, 49, 85
Azarian, Mary, iv, 48

## B
Bauer, Marion Dane, 85, 86
Baylor, Byrd, 60, 61
Begay, Shonto, 50, 87, 88
Billingsley, Franny, 61
Bowen, Fred, 35, 65 (photo)
Brett, Jan, 30, 39, 51, 69, 75 (photo)
Bridwell, Norman, 69
Brown, Craig, iii-iv, 14, 22, 26, 27, 40-1, 45, 71, 79-80
Brown, Craig McFarland. (See Brown, Craig)
Brown, Marc, 13
Brown, Marcia, 20
Bryan, Ashley, iv, 1, 2 (photo), 56 (photo), 57
Bunting, Eve, 29, 49, 57
Burch, Robert, 5
Byars, Betsy, 59, 63, 85

## C
Campbell, Joseph, 27, 28
Carle, Eric, 20, 27, 30, 51, 58 (photo), 59, 87
Carris, Joan, 30
Christelow, Eileen, 28
Cleary, Beverly, 21, 26, 30, 85, 86
Corbett, Scott, 39
Corcoran, Barbara, 21
Crews, Donald, 21
Cummings, Pat, , 60-61
Curtis, Christopher Paul, 58

## D
Danziger, Paula, 9 (photo)
deClements, Barthe, 23
Delton, Judy, 29
dePaola, Tomie, 35, 50, 51, 62
deRegniers, Beatrice Schenk, iv, 4-5, 45, 49, 54
Dillon, Diane, 21, 27
Dillon, Leo, 21, 27
Duffey, Betsy, 63

## E
Ehlert, Lois, 60
Ehrlich, Amy, 31
Emberley, Ed, 21

## F
Freedman, Russell, 20 (photo), 30
Fritz, Jean, 59

## G
Galdone, Paul, 30
Gammell, Stephen, 30. 36-37
Geisel, Theodor Seuss, 87
George, Jean Craighead, 58
Gibbons, Gail, 29, 30
Giblin, James Cross, 21
Goble, Paul, 60
Gorman, Carol, 5, 14, 25 (photo), 38, 58, 69
Griffith, Helen V., 29
Grimes, Nikki, 20

## H
Halloran, Bill, 20
Hamilton, Virginia, 31
Hansen, Jeri, 26
Hermes, Patricia, 38
Hest, Amy, 20
Hobbs, Will, 20
Hopkins, Lee Bennett, 59 (photo)
Hopkinson, Deborah, 61, 63, 86
Howe, James, 60
Hurwitz, Johanna, 23, 60
Hutchins, Pat, 13

## J
Johnson, Steve, 26
Jonas, Ann, 13
Jukes, Mavis, 58

## K
Kasza, Keiko, 45
Kellogg, Steven, 25, 77 (photo)
Kerr, M.E., 58
Kimmel, Eric A., 14, 21, 35, 37 (photo), 50
Kinsey-Warnock, Natalie, 31
Kline, Suzy, 23
Korman, Gordon, 23
Kroll, Steven, 23, 29
Kurtz, Jane, 2, 14, 21 (photo), 62, 64, 86
Kuskin, Karla, 58, 60

## L
L'Engle, Madeleine, 20, 58
Leach, Molly, 26
Leedy, Loreen, 2, 13, 33, 51, 78
Lewis, E. B., 2, 14, 21., 27, 62
Lobel, Arnold, 13, 21
Locker, Thomas, 27
Lowry, Lois, 20

## M
Maesto, Betsy, 23
Maesto, Guilo, 23
Marshall, James, 13, 57
Martin, Jacqueline Briggs, iv, 5, 10 (photo), 21, 48 (photo), 53, 58, 69

Martin, Rafé, 59
McDermott, Gerald, 27, 28, 31
McGovern, Ann, 23
McKissack, Fredrick, 35
McKissack, Patricia, 35, 60
McMillan, Bruce, 23
McPhail, David, 1, 36 (photo)
Meyers, Laurie, 63
Mohr, Nicholasa, 21, 35 (photo)
Mollel, Tolowa, 27
Most, Bernard, 57
Murphy, Stuart, 33

### N
Nixon, Joan Lowery, 21, 39

### O
Okimoto, Jean Davies, 12

### P
Pallotta, Jerry, 29
Parish, Herman, 2
Paterson, Katherine, 21, 85
Paulsen, Gary, 20, 43 (photo)
Peck, Richard, 59
Peet, Bill, 30, 60
Peterson, John, 23
Pfeffer, Susan Beth, 23
Pilkey, Dav, 6, 59
Pinkney, Andrea Davis, 51, 87
Pinkney, Brian, 27, 50, 87
Pinkney, Gloria, 50, 87
Pinkney, Jerry, 27, 50, 57, 87
Pinkwater, Daniel, 48
Polacco, Patricia, 27, 34 (photo), 50, 60
Prelutsky, Jack, 35, 57

### Q
Quackenbush, Robert, 27

### R
Ransome, James, 27, 61
Ringgold, Faith, 60 (photo)
Roberts, Willo Davis, 28, 39
Rubel, Nicole, 61, 87 (photo)
Ryan, Pam Muñoz, 26
Rylant, Cynthia, 6, 29, 30, 57

### S
Sachar, Louis, 23, 61
Sachs, Marilyn, 20, 23, 34
San Souci, Robert, 50
Say, Allen, 20, 21, 27
Schwartz, David, 33
Scieszka, Jon, 26
Seuss, Dr. (See Geisel, Theodor Seuss)
Seuss, Dr., 26
Simon, Seymour, 60
Sis, Peter, 50, 51, 87
Skurzynski, Gloria, 5, 52

Small, David, 21
Smith, Cynthia Leitich, 27 (photo)
Smith, Lane, 26
Smith, Roland, 35
Soto, Gary, 23
Stanley, Diane, 55 (photo)
Steven Kellogg, 28
Stevens, Janet, 37, 62

### T
Taylor, Mildred D., 57
Taylor, Mildred Peck, 27
Terkel, Susan, 23
Thaler, Mike, 22

### U
Uchida, Yoshika, 59

### W
Waber, Bernard, 57
Wells, Rosemary, 76
Werlin, Nancy, 61
Whitney, Thomas P., 54
Wilder, Laura ingalls, 57
Wilhelm, Hans, 23
Willard, Nancy, 29
Wisniewski, David, iv, 1, 2 , 21, 27, 50, 52, 71
Wood, Audrey, 63
Wood, Don, 62-63

### Y
Yolen, Jane, 31, 59

### Z
Zelinsky, Paul O., 23, 24 (photo)

# About the Author

 Sharron L. McElmeel earned a graduate degree in library science from the University of Iowa and has many hours of postgraduate work in reading and curriculum. She is an educator, consultant, and author. In 1997, she was nominated for the Iowa Teacher of the Year honor and previously was named Iowa Reading Teacher of the Year, the only library media specialist to be so honored. Her publications include more than two dozen books for educators, including several for Linworth Publishing. Her articles and author and illustrator profiles are frequently published in *The Book Report* and *Library Talk* (Linworth Publishing, Inc.) as well as in several other publications.